Undrowned

Black Feminist Lessons from Marine Mammals

Undrowned

Black Feminist Lessons from Marine Mammals

Alexis Pauline Gumbs

Foreword by adrienne maree brown

Emergent Strategy Series

AK Press

Undrowned: Black Feminist Lessons from Marine Mammals
Emergent Strategy Series No. 2
© Alexis Pauline Gumbs, 2020
Foreword © adrienne maree brown, 2020
This edition © 2020 AK Press (Chico, Edinburgh)

ISBN: 978-1-84935-397-7
E-ISBN: 978-1-84935-398-4
Library of Congress Control Number: 2020933425

AK Press   AK Press
370 Ryan Ave. #100   33 Tower St.
Chico, CA 95973   Edinburgh EH6 7BN
USA   Scotland
www.akpress.org   www.akuk.com
akpress@akpress.org   akuk@akpress.org

Please contact us to request the latest AK Press distribution catalog, which
features books, pamphlets, zines, and stylish apparel published and/or
distributed by AK Press. Alternatively, visit our websites for the complete
catalog, latest news, and secure ordering.

Cover design by Herb Thornby
Interior design by Margaret Killjoy | birdsbeforethestorm.net
Printed in the USA on acid-free, recycled paper

Dedicated to my ancestral mother Boda, who survived the transatlantic initiation and to you Sangodare, my star at sea

Contents

preface

a guide to undrowning

WHAT IS THE SCALE OF breathing? You put your hand on your individual chest as it rises and falters all day. But is that the scale of breathing? You share air and chemical exchange with everyone in the room, everyone you pass by today. Is the scale of breathing within one species? All animals participate in this exchange of release for continued life. But not without the plants. The plants in their inverse process, release what we need, take what we give without being asked. And the planet, wrapped in ocean breathing, breathing into sky. What is the scale of breathing? You are part of it now. You are not alone.

And if the scale of breathing is collective, beyond species and sentience, so is the impact of drowning. The massive drowning yet unfinished where the distance of the ocean meant that people could become property, that life could be for sale. I am talking about the middle passage and every-one who drowned and everyone who continued breathing. But I am troubling the distinction between the two. I am saying that those who survived in the underbellies of boats, under each other under unbreathable circumstances are the undrowned, and their breathing is not separate from the drowning of their kin and fellow captives, their breathing is not separate from the breathing of the ocean, their breathing is not separate from the sharp exhale of hunted whales, their kindred also. Their breathing did not make them individual survivors. It made a context. The context of undrowning. Breathing in unbreathable circumstances is what we do every day in the chokehold of racial gendered ableist capitalism. We are still undrowning. And by we, I don't only mean people like myself whose ancestors specifically survived the middle passage, because the scale of our breathing is planetary, at the very least.

Are you still breathing? This is an offering towards our evolution, towards the possibility that instead of continuing the trajectory of slavery, entrapment, separation, and domination and making our atmosphere unbreathable, we might instead practice another way to breathe. I don't know what that will look like, but I do know that our marine mammal kindred are amazing at not drowning. So I call on them as teachers, mentors, guides. And I call on you as breathing kindred souls. May we evolve.

foreword

adrienne maree brown

OF COURSE I AM WRITING this on a nineteenth day. and this is a book with nineteen parts. it's a week since I learned nineteen-year-old Black lives matter activist oluwatoyin salai was found dead, and it's quite possible that i have grieved in nineteen ways already today, although this kind of stranger-grief is a difficult thing to track. today i created a meditation of nineteen wisdoms from Black feminists, listening to the throughline between ancestors and living geniuses the way Alexis Pauline Gumbs taught me to do.

and it's not the nineteenth of any month, but of June, June 19th. juneteenth. a day of liberation. given that this is a book of liberation, i wanted to push off into the waters today.

with Alexis things always line up in ways that humble me. grief and magic touch, and a ripple unfolds between them that shows how they are the same thing at different moments in the nonlinear timeline of a good life. the universe is coordinated when it comes around Alexis, because she is steady enough to center any space she enters, however vast. in the pages that follow, she is leading us through oceans, inviting us to grab onto her fin as she takes us deep and teaches us how and when to breathe, how to handle the pressure of depth, where to leap and catch the sun's light.

when Alexis first started posting these marine mammal missives, i thought—oh, emergent strategy from the deep. this is a whole realm of the wild world that i have barely gotten to learn from, and that has a huge amount to teach us right now on how we survive, how we slow down, how we make the air last, how we avoid predation and extinction, how we play.

i have always felt myself to be a child of the ocean, but like many Black humans, the lines that tether me to distinct Earth and water were cut long ago. with *Undrowned*, Alexis offers back to us a set of ancestors, sibling species, a variety of solidarities that can teach me about myself. i didn't know i had so much Blackness in common with the marine mammal world! this text feels like meeting an eccentric and wise and intriguing family. it feels like an unveiling, Alexis pulling up the salt skirt of sea to show us how we belong, how we are echoes of the same brilliance as dolphins and seals and whales.

i am so grateful that Alexis wrote this down, and that she is letting us publish it as the first comrade text in the Emergent Strategy Series at AK Press. i hope you find a multitude of teachings in these pages, as i did, and that this work deepens your life as it has mine.

adrienne maree brown
from the realm of pandemics and uprisings
6/19/2020

introduction

IF YOU HAPPEN TO BE in the ocean and you see someone breathing, what do you do? If you see someone like you, a mammal, but unlike you—not bound by boats and masks and land—you might wonder who they are, what they are doing, how do they do it. How do they live in salt and depth and motion? You very well might wonder. And in that case you would need a guidebook. The most available guidebooks around right now are the *National Audubon Society Guide to Marine Mammals of the World* and the *Smithsonian Handbook: Whales, Dolphins & Porpoises*. They will summarize the available scientific information on the habitats, habits, and appearances of all the animals they have tracked so you can identify a mammal, and later, when you get out of the ocean, tell someone who you saw.

I identify *as* a mammal. I identify as a Black woman ascending with and shaped by a whole group of people who were transubstantiated into property and kidnapped across an ocean. And, like many of us, I am simply attracted to the wonder of marine life. And so I went to the aquarium and bought both of those guidebooks hoping to learn about my kin.

What I found was that the languages of deviance and denigration (for example, the term "vagrant juveniles," used to describe hooded seals), awkwardly binary assignments of biological sex, and a strange criminalization of mammals that escaped the gaze of biologists showed up in what would call itself the "neutral" scientific language of marine guidebooks. I just wanted to know which whale was which, but I found myself confronted with the colonial, racist, sexist, heteropatriachalizing capitalist constructs that are trying to kill me—the net I am already caught in, so to speak. So how can I tell you who and what I saw?

At the same time, as I learned more about marine mammals, I learned to look between the loopholes of language, using the poetic practices I have had to use to find and love myself in a world that misnames me daily. And I felt so much love and humility. I felt so much awe and possibility. I had to show you what I felt. So I posted on social media every day what I was learning about marine mammals, from and despite the guidebooks, through my own further research, afro-futuristic speculation, and what was happening to my heart.

Instead of simply identifying what was what, I had to go deeper. I took my cue from the many marine mammals who echolocate. I had to focus not on what I could see and discern, but instead on where I was in relation, how the sound bouncing off me in relationship to the structures and environments that surround me locates me in a constantly shifting relationship to you, whoever you are by now.

As I continued to post what I was learning, my Instagram followers spiked, people gave me watercolor journals of whales,[1] mailed me knitted humpback earrings,[2] sent me the actual vertebrae of a whale (for real!),[3] and more. I also got messages online every day asking when and where they could buy these reflections in a book, offering to be my research

1   Thank you Solanke Omimuyegun!
2   Thank you Natalie Clark!
3   Thank you Tema Okun!

assistant, testifying that these posts had become their daily meditations and offering to collaborate on creating apps, song-based audio meditations, and one special message from adrienne suggesting that these writings could be a part of the Emergent Strategy imprint/bookflow/paradigm at AK Press. And here we are.

So this is a different kind of guidebook for our movements and our whole species based on the subversive and transformative guidance of marine mammals. Where Emergent Strategy offers us the opportunity to study and practice the work of shaping change by understanding ourselves as part of the ongoing emergence of nature, this guide to undrowning listens to marine mammals specifically as a form of life that has much to teach us about the vulnerability, collaboration, and adaptation we need in order to be with change at this time, especially since one of the major changes we are living through, causing, and shaping in this climate crisis is this rising of the ocean. And the other is that a pandemic that emerged while I was sending back copyedits for this book also threatens our breath.

I don't see this book as a critique of the two guidebooks I mentioned. I see this book as an offering to you and as an artifact of a process I am in the midst of called *Marine Mammal Apprenticeship.* If there was ever a time to humbly submit to the mentorship of marine mammals it is now. Did I mention the ocean is rising? Have you noticed the adaptation in our breathing? This is a pragmatic course of study. At the same time, part of what is at stake for me in this apprenticeship is a transformed relationship to my own breathing, the salt-water within me, the depth of my grief, and the leagues of my love. And in order to have space for the relationship to the learning and unlearning that is necessary for me in this process, I have to do some work to disrupt the violent colonizing languages of almost all the texts in which I have accessed information about marine mammals and their lives, and families and super-powers and struggles.

The Audubon and Smithsonian guidebooks are the sources of all unattributed quotations in this book, and I often start the meditations mimicking the cadence of objectivity that guidebook entries perform. I'm doing that on purpose, I want to remember it's a performance and then I want to transform it. Though I usually avoid the passive voice because it hides accountability (I've written about this elsewhere),[4] in this text the passive voice is a major mimicking device of the scientific forms of writing, which teach scientists to use the passive voice in order to take themselves out of the intimacy of their research towards the illusion of objectivity. Nothing is objective. And think about it, scientists, especially those people who have designed their entire lives around the hope, the possibility that they will encounter a marine mammal, and who have taken extreme measures (like moving to Antarctica) in order to increase the likelihood that they will see some particular marine being, cannot be unmoved. They are clearly obsessed, and most likely, like me, in love. Whether they can admit it in their publications or not.[5]

In this book I move, mostly without warning, from a clinical tone to a profoundly intimate tone. The words "I love you" appear more than any other phrase in this book. I'm sure those words have never appeared in scientific studies about marine mammals.[6] My hope, my grand poetic intervention here is to move from identification, also known as that process through which we say what is what, like which dolphin is that over there and what are its properties, to *identification*, that process through which we expand our empathy and the boundaries of who we are become more fluid, because we *identify with* the experience of someone different,

---

4   See Alexis Pauline Gumbs, "The Problem With the Passive Past Tense," in *Black Perspectives*, July 10, 2018. https://www.aaihs.org/the-problem-with-the-passive-past-tense/.

5   I recently facilitated a writing workshop with scientists at Cal Tech inviting them to put themselves, their passions, and their relationships back into their writing about their research topics, and I would love to do this again. Scientists, let's collaborate!

6   But if you have read that study, please send it to me!

maybe someone of a whole different so-called species. This is a tricky task because I'm vulnerable, not only to the messiness of my emotions, but also to the possibility of just projecting onto a whole set of beings who can't verbally protest my projections. And though the systems of oppression that harm me also harm advanced marine mammals (I am a beginner marine mammal very early in my journey), we are not having the same experience. In other words, this is not a book in which I am trying to garner sympathy for marine mammals because they are so much like us (though we do have things in common). Instead, the intimacy, the intentional ambiguity about who is who, speaking to whom and when is about undoing a definition of the human, which is so tangled in separation and domination that it is consistently making our lives incompatible with the planet.

My task here, as a marine mammal apprentice, opening myself to guidance from these advanced marine mammals is to identify *with*. To see what happens when I rethink and refeel my own relations, possibilities, and practices inspired by the relations, possibilities, and practices of advanced marine mammal life. That's an emergent strategy. If interlocking underground communication of trees, dandelion resilience, and responsive mycelium networks can inspire us to relate within and across species differently so can marine mammals. And emergent for real. I am mostly asking questions of myself and of you in this text. We get to continue to consider what is possible from here (and here and here).

And since I can't help but notice how marine mammals are queer, fierce, protective of each other, complex, shaped by conflict, and struggling to survive the extractive and militarized context our species has imposed on the ocean and ourselves, this work is accountable to the movements that are boldly seeking to transform the meaning of life on the planet right now. Movements for Black liberation, queer liberation, disability justice, economic justice, racial justice, and gender justice are core to the meditations that are included here. But these are still meditations. Instead of proposing a specific agenda or a predetermined set of instructions, these meditations open up space for wondering together and asking questions towards a depth of engagement that is, yes, still emerging.

The book consists of an introduction and nineteen thematic movements (it would be too linear to say "chapters" and, anyway, they are much shorter than chapters) organized around core Black feminist practices like breathing, remembering, collaborating, etc., as they can be informed and transformed by learning from marine mammals (and a couple of sharks). Some of the hashtags I originally used for these pieces on social media remain as references and citations. It closes with a movement called "activation" that offers some guided group and individual activities for you to do with the meditations in the book.

Did I Introduce Myself?

Oh right. I'm a queer Black feminist love evangelist and a marine mammal apprentice. All of my formal education and most of my mentorships have been squarely in the arena of queer Black feminism. My poetic academic works—*Spill: Scenes of Black Feminist Fugitivity*, *M Archive: After the End of the World*, and *Dub: Finding Ceremony*—all bring the work of Black feminist theorists (and high theorists at that) into the accessible (but still complicated and mysterious) realms of community memory, visionary futures, and ancestral listening. My movement writing, most notably *Revolutionary Mothering: Love on the Front Lines* (PM Press, 2016), which I co-edited alongside Mai'a Williams and China Martens; my years writing for *Make/Shift* and *Left Turn* magazines; and my many contributions to AK Press books (*Pleasure Activism, Stay Solid, Dear Sister, Feminisms in Motion, Octavia's Brood*, etc.) also draws on archives of Black feminist practice to nourish the bravery we need right now. My creative writing spans from poetry to visionary fiction, like the story "Evidence" in *Octavia's Brood*, which imagines a future researcher studying "the time of the silence breaking" and how the world, free of sexual violence, that they live in came to be, or "Bluebellow" in *Strange Horizons*, which imagines mermaid zombie survivors of the middle passage connecting with Black people who take a reverse transatlantic journey to Europe.

My movement work has focused on poetry, ceremony, and facilitation. As a founding member of UBUNTU, a women of color survivor-led coalition to end gendered violence and create sustaining transformative love and Earthseed People of Color Land Collective in Durham, NC; a member leader of Southerners on New Ground; a member of the founding vision circle of Kindred Healing Justice; a founding member of the transformative local foundation Warrior Healers Organizing Trust; and a member of SpiritHouse, my participation in movement is accountable to Black queer visionaries in the US South and beyond. As founder of Eternal Summer of the Black Feminist Mind, Brilliance Remastered, and co-founder of Black Feminist Bookmobile, Black Feminist Film School, and the Mobile Homecoming—an experiential archive of Black queer brilliance—I am committed to creating counter-institutions that facilitate Black feminist presence across time and space.

What is the ecology?

This book already exists in an ecology of kindred works. First of all I exist in the ecology of my Shinnecock ancestors who have been in sacred relationship with the Atlantic Right Whale for centuries and my Ashanti ancestors who call the name of the whale as one of the names of god. And my grandmother Lydia Gumbs created the three dolphin insignia for the revolutionary flag of Anguilla during the 1967 revolution. Certainly this work is a baby cousin of *Emergent Strategy* and has been nurtured by the revolutionary and humble approach to learning from nature modeled by my dear sister adrienne there. In fact, I first shared these posts in the Emergent Strategy group on facebook. The great movement folk singer Toshi Reagon also facilitated audio versions of eleven of these meditations and composed incredible songs that will be released together as "Long Water Song." This practice was influenced by my daily engagement with Sharon Bridgforth's oceanic oracles, the *dat Black Mermaid Man Lady* oracle deck, and *dem blessings*, the companion series of oceanic compassion prompts. Every day those oracles set the tone for my deep listening. At the end of each post I encouraged readers to support my dear sister collaborator Michaela Harrison's *Whale Whispering Project,* a Black feminist collaboration Michaela designed with the Humpback Whale Institute in Bahia, Brazil, through which she co-writes songs with whales using underwater microphone technology. The approach to life science that emerged for me in this process is also deeply informed by my dear sister (and fellow UBUNTU founding member) Kriti Sharma, the biologist and philosopher who wrote the book *Interdependence*. On one of Kriti's first deep sea voyages, she sent a cup with a prayer for all beings to the bottom of the ocean. The pressure of the ocean compressed the cup and she brought that compressed prayer back for me. The cup has been on my altar ever since. Right now Kriti is in Pasadena (Octavia Butler's home and final resting place), studying how sediment at the bottom of the ocean processes methane. She may be right now discovering the key to reversing global warming! Also the seeds of this process came from the historian Charles McKinney who taught a group of gifted eleven- and twelve-year-olds about the Middle Passage by assigning us to read the scene in Octavia Butler's *Wild Seed* where the protagonist jumps off of an enslaving vessel and becomes a dolphin. Clearly I am still gratefully inside of that assignment. I am also influenced and inspired by my kindred spirit dreamer, self-identified ocean creature Tala Khanmalek, the founder of Sailing for Social Justice, who is imagining oceanic justice through revolutionary sailing. This kinship with ocean animals is also inspired by my twin portal Leah Lakshmi-Piepzna Samarasinha and the *Femme Shark* collective's zines and manifesta, as well as Qwo-li Driscoll's *Bull Shark*

Manifesto. And as you will soon see, a few sharks even snuck their way into this marine mammal journey.

Who is this book for?

This book is for you! Also known as everyone who knows that a world where queer Black feminine folks are living their most abundant, expressed, and loving lives is a world where everyone is free. I imagine that most people will not read the book front to back, but I have still organized it based on the Black feminist/marine mammal principle of flow, just in case. I imagine that folks will work with one meditation at a time as part of a daily meditation practice. So far people have shared with me that they have excerpted these meditations during their own keynote lectures, used them as a way to start the day, used them to launch writing prompts of their own, and shared them with friends as love letters and accountability reminders. I wrote this with you in mind, you comrades who go to the Allied Media Conference, who used to read *Make/Shift* and *Left Turn*, and use social media fluently. I wrote this with you in mind, dreamers that live near the shore and wonder about the whale bones you find. I wrote this with you in mind, those of you lobbying at the United Nations about deep ocean ecology and what it takes to honor it. And you, the ones who can't keep from crying when you read the daily news. And you, the ones who feel cut off from nature. And you, the people who prioritize nature in your lives. And us, the people who are anxious about climate crisis. Us, the people who take long social media fasts and want peace. Yes, you and me, the ones who thought our practice of looking at pictures of marine mammals was completely separate from our economic justice work. This is for all of us. You are on my mind and in my heart.

The word "Black" is capitalized throughout this text. Thanks to the work of Black writers and editors over decades the convention is that usually the word Black is capitalized when it refers to Black people and lowercase when it refers to Black as a color or adjective. But Blackness is more expansive than the human. And there is no symbolic or descriptive reference to the term Black in this society that does not also impact Black lives. So Black is Black.

one

listen

How can we listen across species, across extinction, across harm? How does echolocation, the practice many marine mammals use to navigate the world through bouncing sounds, change our understandings of "vision" and visionary action? Is social media already a technology of bounce, of throwing something out there and seeing what comes back?

This is where we start our trans-species communion, opening a space to uplift the practice of listening even more than the practices of showing and proving and speaking up. Listening is not only about the normative ability to hear, it is a transformative and revolutionary resource that requires quieting down and tuning in.

Once upon a time there was a giant sea mammal, who weighed up to twenty-three tons, swimming in the Bering Sea. In 1741, a German naturalist "discovered" *Hydrodamalis gigas* swimming large and luxe, at least three times bigger than the contemporary manatee. Within twenty-seven years, the entire species was extinct, killed on thousands of European voyages for fur and sealskin.

So she knows what we know. It is dangerous to be discovered.

Twenty-seven years. Who else could only tolerate twenty-seven years among western humans? Jimi Hendrix, Jean-Michel Basquiat, even Amy Winehouse, and Kurt Cobain. Twenty-seven years is such a short time. How do we mourn and survive the violence of being known? How does capitalism so quickly destroy what took billions of years to evolve?

What do we know about this subungulate mammal, related to elephants and aardvarks?

She had blubber and was hunted for it. They say she couldn't sing. The only sound was her breathing, but she could hear for miles and miles and miles. What a loss for listening. How can we honor it, the archive of your breathing?

Some say your death was only incidental; you were so conveniently located on the favorite path of sealers and fur traders between Russia and North America. Those twenty-seven years were like a gold rush, fueled by the desires of fashionable Europeans for fur hats and coats. A fashion trend sparked by colonizing North America: a supposedly endless supply of fur. They were on their way to get sealskin and fur. They would kill you and eat you during the journey there. Does that make anyone feel better? Keep anyone warm? That your extinction—the first known extinction of a marine mammal caused by humans—was collateral in the pursuit of other deaths?

Oh you rough mermaid, what are you teaching us about breath? Oh massive vegetarian, what do we do now that our listening is that much smaller? I think you are more than evidence of the deadliness of a world in which skin is for sale at a premium. I think you are more than another testament of the stark implications of European voyaging. More than an indictment of the rush. More than the folly of a dominant way of living that changes the planet, quickly, thoughtlessly, forever. More than the deadliness of an insatiable hunger born of chasing things other than sustenance. That hunger outlived you. I feel it chasing me too.

What can I do to honor you, now that it is too late?

I would honor you with the roughness of my skin, the thickness of my boundaries, the warmth of my own fat. I would honor you with my quiet and my breathing, my listening further and further out and in. I would honor you with the slowness of my movement, contemplative and graceful. I would try to be like you even though they say it's out of fashion. I will remember you. Not by the name (written in the possessive) of the one they say "discovered" you after generations of Indigenous relationship.

I will say *once upon a time there was a huge and quiet swimmer, a plant-based rough-skinned listener, a fat and graceful mammal.* And then I will be quiet, so I can hear you breathing. And then I will be breathing and you'll remind me, do not rush. And the time in me will hush. And then we will be listening for real.

In the past twenty years, bioacoustic scientists have spent a lot of time listening to different populations of Indo-Pacific bottlenose dolphins. These dolphins, like most dolphins, know something about intentional sound. About when to use high frequencies to find out where they are, and when to use low frequencies to reach you across this increasing ambient noise. Echolocation and communication overlap but they also diverge. Sometimes the sounds I make are about measuring my surroundings. Sometimes there is something

I need to tell you. Usually it's both. Dolphins use the fat in their foreheads to modulate their biosonar listening, which sounds about as elegant as what I do with you.

Sometimes I feel like I'm communicating with you underwater. The impact of what I say outlives what I learned by saying it. And the ambient noise grows louder and the ocean is heating up and I need you to know where the bottom is, what will feed us, how close are the sharks. Sometimes my best guess echoes back to me like a slap in the face and I remember I know nothing. This fat forehead needs you and all your guesses too in this dynamic space.

Which is to say I am humbly listening and I am learning to take responsibility for my frequencies. I can lower them to reach you. I can reflect before I speak out. Echolocation is not the same as mind-reading. Some of this magic is just the complexity of being a mammal alive in sound. I can hear what I cannot see yet. I can make a whole world of resonance. And live in it. Swim through it. Reflecting you. Whistle, click if you can feel that I am here.

They say river dolphins don't leap as much as dolphins in the ocean. Because of turbid flows of rushing water, they do not trust their eyes. Their eyes grow small. Echolocation becomes crucial. Their listening becomes more nuanced. They become experts of shape, and shape themselves to become narrow, reaching forward like the river. River dolphins all over the world (in the Ganges and Amazon rivers for example) are not close genetic relatives. But they are remarkably physically similar. They have grown common forms due to their common circumstances.

Have you grown that way, riverine? In a context that moves so quickly that looking at it tells you almost nothing.

Are you evolving a deeper way of listening where you are? Could we become students of shape precise enough to move with the grace and flexibility our circumstance requires even though your river is not my river?

I am amazed by how much listening can do. How quickly it becomes less important to be seen, to leap, to show. And those who study river dolphins know it too. Don't bother looking for these teachers who will rarely jump or splash. You have to listen for them, try to hear them breathe.

I breathe in shape. I shape my days while land contours me at two sides. I shape my breath to wind through winding paths ahead. I shape my head to fit the purpose of my breath. My breath is prayer, the shape of life, evolving name. All I can see is just the blur that says life moves. I stay in prayer, and reach to listen for your breath.

There is a dolphin found only on the shores of Aotearoa, that the Māori sometimes call "tūpoupou." Which also means to rise up, to toss and turn, to be seriously ill. Word is, Māori meteorologists have been studying these dolphins for centuries to gain insights about the weather. What we might have to endure and how soon. And should we go out to sea or stay in? And will the sky fall on us yet? And where will the wind take us?

Western scientists have classified the leaping of tūpoupou in three ways: horizontal, vertical, and noisy. Noisy means you land on your side, on your back, on your belly; you rise up, toss and turn, and for a moment, when you fall, the ocean is a drum. And someone is listening, because how you move, how you land is a sign of the weather to come.

And you rise up. And you fall loudly. And you toss and turn. And something about this climate makes you sick, doesn't it? And I am listening too. Because of what you do and its direction. How you fall and the sound. Where you go and how quickly. These tell me something about what is coming in a sky I can't see yet.

And I love you for all of your splashing. What you did with your body, how you made it a drum. And I say your play and your thrash are prophetic. And I say your name is a verb, a demand. And I offer my days to your urgent instruction. The weather is changing. Yes. I understand.[7]

---

7 #weatherandwake #thankyouchristinasharpe

two

breathe

BREATH IS A PRACTICE OF presence. One of the physical char-acteristics that unites us with marine mammals is that they process air in a way similar to us. Though they spend most or all of their time in water, they do not have gills. We, too, on land are often navigating contexts that seem impossible for us to breathe in, and yet we must. The adaptations that marine mammals have made in relationship to breathing are some of the most relevant for us to observe, not only in rela-tionship to our survival in an atmosphere we have polluted on a planet where we are causing the ocean to rise, but also in relationship to our intentional living, our mindful relation to each other.

With meditations on the different ways that narwhal, be-luga, and bowhead whales breathe in the Arctic, the ways baby seals learn to redefine breath in infancy, the relationship between the endangered North Atlantic right whale and my Shinnecock and enslaved ancestors, and even a surprise visit by a Blacktip reef shark, this section offers us opportunities to look at what blocks our breathing, and the stakes of a society that puts profit over breath. May our breathing open up to the possibility of peace.

There is more than one way to breathe in the Arctic. Ask the narwhal, beluga, and bowhead whales.

Beluga shapeshifts, evolved to look like ice itself, and congregates in the shallow estuaries, singing.

Narwhal stays in deeper water, nearer to pack ice, grows a horn to break through, changes color over its life. Needs no other teeth. Just the one.

Bowhead says bigger is better and moves alone. Strong enough to break ice with a bare skull, old enough to remember before all of this. Never stops growing.

And you? Maybe it's time to remember that there is more than one way to breathe in icy depths or summer heat. To thank your ancestors for how you have evolved in the presence of polar bears, harpoons, and other threats. To think on what you want to shift, how you want to grow, what you need to remember.

And me? It was always you I loved, not your elegant strategy. I will love you still, if you now outgrow it. I will love you more whether time moves forward or backwards. Whether ice melts or water freezes back. Whether your next move is protection, breakthrough, shift, or any combination. There are at least three ways to love you: as you were, as you are, as you will be. I love you. That means I choose all three.

The baby Weddell seal has not grown into her flippers. She is awkward. She does not want to swim. She does not know she can breathe underwater. No one has told her about the great oxygenating capacity of her blood. She doesn't know that the milk her mother gives her is some of the fat-richest milk in the world. Southernmost mammal on the planet, she doesn't know the depths of which she is capable. But her mother does.

The mother Weddell seal will push her baby into the water against her will. She will force her child's head into the water while the baby coughs and sputters and struggles and squirms. She is new here. She does not know that she can breathe underwater. Until she does. And then everything changes. By the time weaning is over she will be able to dive 2,500 feet below the water. Stay there for an hour if she wants to. Find a tiny hole she made for air after swimming twelve kilometers away. Move gracefully between frozen and liquid worlds. But she doesn't know.

Am I the only one here in a lesson, a coughing sputtering thrash, a struggle to stay who I thought I was, ignorant to what evolution has already written inside me? I feel out of my depth, but really, how would I know?

The tough love of the Weddell seal mother teaches a lesson about the difference between what is cute and what is necessary. What has been and what could be. And I am grateful for all of my mothers, biological, chosen and ancestral, mammal and otherwise (like the copperhead snake who greeted me last night), who would shock me into knowing my capacity, trust my lungs more than I thought I could. To breathe in ways I haven't breathed before. To learn my blood in ways I didn't know it.

As the Weddell seal grows she will shed her fur, become sleek. She will feel completely at home in the ocean she avoided. She will see and feel things no other mammal has felt. But right now she is coughing and spitting and clinging to what she has known. She feels like she is drowning, but she's just meeting herself again for the first time.

Love to all my parents and the push of the universe for laughing at me. Thank you to those of you who have pushed through portals already, even out of this life. We can move between worlds. Thank you for those of you living and evolving, the vulnerability of your newness is an example to us all. Thank you to those who hold me accountable, who expect me to be who I need to become. Thank you for ignoring the lies I tell myself about myself. Even in my resistance I am grateful for you all. For the love you are teaching me, deep, Black, and full. For the nurturance, push, and example. What you learned by facing your own death. What you learned in your drowning is my breath.[8]

The second I set foot on the beach at Bridgehampton, a whale surfaced and exhaled. From where I stood, on occupied sacred Shinnecock land, I couldn't see whether it was a fin whale or a humpback whale, but in my heart I thought maybe, just maybe it was a North Atlantic right whale. The right whale, the rarest whale in the ocean, hunted nearly into extinction to (literally) fuel the colonial project. Blubber and light.

Used to be a right whale could breathe for a century. Now that never happens. They rarely live five years without scars from boat propellers, rope wounds from tangled commerce. And it's not necessary. Boats could shift or slow their paths quite easily. You know what is necessary? Breath. Theirs more so than ours, truth be told. Yesterday I learned that the breathing of whales is as crucial to our own breathing and the carbon cycle of the planet as are the forests of the world. Researchers say, if whales returned to their pre-commercial whaling numbers, their gigantic breathing would store as much carbon as 110,000 hectares of forest, or a forest the size of Rocky Mountain National Park.

The Shinnecock, now and since forever, including some of my ancestors, are in sacred relationship with the North Atlantic right whale. A listening that spans centuries. Once the beaching of a right whale was an offering to the whole community. Nourishment and light. Shelter and warmth.

---

8   #docjosephriseinpower

But that day on the shoreline, the poet Kathy Engel told me she had never seen a whale in all her sixty years of growing up at that beach until just this summer. *Did you call them with your writing?* She asked me online.

Yes. I have been calling you forever. With my blood and with my breathing. I remember what you gave us which is everything. Light, home, and each other. Love, warmth, and ourselves. If I breathe, I sing your name. I can only breathe because of you. Do you have a century more of breath? And if not, what do I have?

Home is light but loss is heavy. And I cannot live without you. Why would I want to live without you? Steward of centuries, transformer of air, I ever await your message and assignment. In debt and gratitude, in trust and tide. I see you. I hear you. I know. I dedicate my breathing to the depth you taught. Are teaching.

"You're welcome."

This is what the young Blacktip reef shark who came right up to the shore and accompanied me on the rest of my walk said.

"What are you doing here?" I asked, in return. "Everyone knows I'm writing about marine mammals, not sharks. And is this even part of your range?"

She took a deep breath under the water. I was jealous. Maybe I do need gills, I thought. But I didn't say...

"First of all," she said, "that's no way to greet a requiem shark. Do you know who my cousins are?" Good point. Tiger shark and them...some of the baddest. But by how she rolled her eyes I could tell she wasn't exactly making a threat. Was I making the wrong assumption?

"Much respect," I said at last.

"What was that? The surf is loud. You know my ears are embedded…"

"MUCH RESPECT!" I repeated. "Much respect, shark of the live birth who breathes underwater, born whole in yourself in the color of sand. Guardian of the reef with your beautiful Black edges. Breaching brown genius, brave even among sharks. That you show yourself ever is a gift to sky. That you showed yourself to me is more than can be expected. I am at your service. I am in your debt. What can I offer?"

"Okay. That's more like it. May you please soon outgrow those limits that do nothing to protect you. And also pass on this message…You're welcome."

*

Three Lies About Sharks That Humans Have Used to Justify Their Own Violence and Alienation that Sharks Will No Longer Tolerate:

1. Sharks travel alone. Translation: Cultivate your sharp individuality. (Not so. The Blacktip reef shark, for example, is highly social, finds safety in numbers. Community is the stronger approach.)

2. Sharks are powerful and effective because they hide. Translation: No one will love you if they see all of who you are. (Not so. For example, Blacktip reef sharks jump out of the water and flip in the air four times even while hunting. You are fierce from every angle.)

3. Sharks spend more time sharpening their teeth than opening their gills. (Do you need a translation here? Breathe.)

*

And an addendum from me:

When even sharks tell you to give peace a chance, you know something has to change. And here are some things I am willing to give up, an offering towards our evolution: the sharpness of knowing who I am, the weapons I filled my mouth with on purpose, the ways I showed only the tip of me when you needed my wholeness the whole time, the lies I let live in my name, the ways I devalued my breathing.

I love each of you for stretching your cartilage and

opening your gills. Thank you for remembering the ancient rule of cycles that the sharks are still protecting. And what a celebration when we realize that our survival need not make us into monsters. When we forgive ourselves for shredding what could never even hurt us. When we evolve in our assignment of brave guardian vulnerability. We have wondered at the sharpness of teeth, glorified the extremes of alienation. We have fetishized exactly what we fear. And now we are here to notice the miracle that was there the entire time. The gills, the permeability of strength. The gills, the way all life is flowing through you. Your breathing. It is your breathing that we need.[9]

---

9   #nomammalsupremacy #oceaniclove #realsharkfriendsdroppingknowledge
    And for more on the queer transformative impact of the shark family, please look to my cherished fam Leah Lakshmi Piepzna-Samarasinha and the "Femme Shark Manifesto!": http://www.qzap.org/v5/gallery/main.php?g2_view=core.DownloadItem&g2_itemId=799.
    And shout out to Qwo-Li Driskill's divine "Bull Shark Manifesto" as well!

three

remember

WHAT DO WE REMEMBER AND what do we forget? How do we name and categorize what we can barely observe, for what purpose, with what results? For example, there is only one marine mammal that the dominant scientific community calls by their Indigenous name. There are supposedly impossible hybrid dolphins along the route of the triangular transatlantic traffic trail of captive human cargo that defy species. There is a battle for the domain name "amazon" in which a huge corporation has more leverage than the ancient rain forest, a whole region of the planet.

What do we need to remember that will push back against the forgetting encouraged by consumer culture and linear time? What can we remember that will surround us in oceans of history and potential? And how?

Once upon a time, I thought the name "Amazon" belonged to Black lesbians. Then I learned that the Amazon was a specific place storied around the world by colonizers who were afraid of the fierceness of the people who would not conform to their ideas about gender and land. I continued to rejoice. And to identify.

As of this writing, the giant retailer that doesn't even have to be named may be about to win a lawsuit for the domain name "amazon." A lawsuit against the rainforest itself. The whole geographic region. Wasn't it only in 2018 that Colombia acknowledged that a rainforest has rights?

And guess what, the only dolphin—and, I believe, the only marine mammal at all—who has managed to keep her Indigenous given name lives in the Amazon. Tuxuci, named in the Tupi language, has kept her name through all this colonization, while most other marine mammals are named after a colonizer at worst and hailed by a bland western description at best. It's a miracle. We say her name.

This is my prayer. May anyone who seeks to mention you be called to learn the language of those who first loved you. May you study the pink of yourself. Know yourself riverine and coast. May you taste the fresh and the saltwater of yourself and know what only you can know. May you live in the mouth of the river, meeting place of the tides, may all blessings flow through you.

I love you impossible dolphin, quietest in the river, breathing close to the surface. I'm grateful for what you remember even if you never say. And I'm keeping your name in my mouth like a river internal, like this love ever flowing. I am keeping your name in my mouth every day. All day.[10]

In 2016, reports circulated with evidence that dolphin mothers sing to their babies while they are in the womb, and for a few weeks after so they can learn their names. Not only that, but according to the report, the rest of the pod holds space for that learning, quieting their other usual sounds so this can happen.[11]

Several loved ones have sent me the articles that share this information. And as a person whose mother sang and talked to me before I was born, it resonates. And interestingly enough this new research was shared, according to these articles, not at a meeting of marine biologists, but at the American Psychological Association meeting in Denver in August 2016. The article never mentions the species of dolphin. This is something that it would feel so good to generalize. As mammals, it would satisfy a deep longing to be part of a practice of mother–child singing, community listening. Held. Named.

Held. Deep diving, as I often do, I learned that the observations leading to this insight about mother/baby womb singing were observed in a specific context. Captivity. A mother dolphin who gave birth at Six Flags Discovery Kingdom. From the pictures I would say a bottlenose dolphin, but even the website doesn't name the species. It matters to me that this practice of singing, communal listening, was observed not in the open ocean but in the confines of captive dolphin birth. I think of Debbie Africa, who gave birth secretly in prison, how the other women prisoners used sounds to shield her birth process. They protected the two of them from guards so that she and the baby were able to share precious time together, undetected for days. I think of Assata Shakur too, impossibly conceiving and giving birth to her daughter while a political prisoner, mostly in solitary confinement.

---

11 See many articles including Stephanie Pappas, "Mama Dolphins Sing to their Babies in the Womb" in *LiveScience*, August 9, 2016, https://www.livescience.com/55699-mother-dolphins-teach-babies-signature-whistle.html.

And how she listened to her angry daughter, and the dreams of her grandmother when they told her she could be free. They could be together. And a community of freedom fighters made the demand and the dream real.

I think of captive birth, which is an everyday occurrence in the United States of America. In the US, the state shackles prisoners giving birth, and takes children away from prisoners almost immediately. What do they sing in the time of the womb? I think of the children of asylum seekers separated from their parents in cages at the border. How does a chorus of grief and loss evolve to share crucial information? How are the over five million US children with parents in prison, the uncounted children in cages at the border, held? Named?

And I think about you and what you remember. What you keep close for as long as you can. I think about repetition and code, and when we prioritize what communication and why. And how we ever learn our names in this mess. And the need that makes us generalize and identify. Become specific and vague. I think about the dolphin mother and what she needed to say. Her own name, in her own way. And what else under strict observation?

If it was me. If it was you. I would say this in the way I could say it, in the too short time, in the high-pitched emergence. Remember this feeling, there is something called love. I would say remember, there is something called freedom, even if you can't see it. There is me calling you, in a world I don't control. There is something called freedom, and you know how to call it. Even here in the holding pattern, here in the hold, remember remember. You are. You are held. Named.

Have you heard about Clymene? A popular name in Greek mythology (and the hair weave and wig marketplace, apparently), Clymene is also the name of the dolphin at the forefront of the minds of marine biologists studying hybridity.

Who is she? A dolphin who escaped the record, only identified as a species in 1981. Mistranscribed when Europeans first identified her in the 1800s and then dismissed as a false identification. What is her range? The shape and trajectory of the transatlantic slave trade, West Africa to the Caribbean and North and South America. Height? About the height of a stolen person. Weight? About the weight of a stolen person.

The Clymene dolphin moves in revolutions like a spinner dolphin. She has a Black cape like a striped dolphin. Where did she come from? Her origins are elusive. Genetic testing of her skin about five years ago in Portugal found that, depending on how they approached the research, they got different results. Quantum skin? Particle genes?

When they did nuclear genetic testing, it seemed the Clymene dolphin was more closely related to the spinner dolphin, but when they tested the mitochondrial DNA (tracing only the maternal line), they found Clymene was more closely related to the striped dolphin. What happened?

The theory now is that she's both. The Clymene dolphin is a hybrid of the spinner and the striped dolphin and therefore may be the most recent dolphin to evolve into existence. And while usually a hybrid form would have to be isolated from the parent species to retain its distinct features, Clymene has somehow, done this while swimming all the time in pods with Striped and Spinner dolphins, but giving birth as Clymene over and over again. Her revolutions. Her Black cape. Sometimes you need both. Her corkscrew turns, her Black lips, spinning from West Africa to the New World, hidden in plain sight for centuries.

My grandfather once told me he identified with Atlas, son of the mythical Oceanid Clymene. Sky on his shoulders. Burdened. Strong. The other young people in Anguilla used to call him "World," and maybe that's the riddle. If Atlas stood at the edge of the world and held up the heavens so the Earth wouldn't break, what did my grandfather find at the edge of himself that was so heavy or heavenly or starred? What did he learn from his mother, grandchild of shipwreck, about the edge of the world or the end? Here, on a particular edge of the Caribbean Sea, a curve in Anguilla they call Rendezvous Bay, ancient site of transient Arawak ceremony, stewarded this half century by my family of origin sometimes with grace, my grandfather taught me to float on my back. He said look at the sky. This is where I still come to look for him. That sky is where I see him in my dreams. I am still learning to trust that something can hold me.

My default mode is burdened strength.

Atlas, Titan, son of the Oceanid Clymene, father of Calypso is an interesting referent for a young man on a small island. The 2019 Junior King of Calypso, Super Mario, won the annual competition with a song about the neglected youth of Anguilla, which was centered around the question "Who's looking out for me?" I guess Super Mario, the heroic plumber, Italian immigrant brother is an interesting referent too. I think my grandfather, who grew up a so-called "illegitimate" child, wearing clothes his mother made out of flour sacks could probably relate. How strong do we have to be? Does it have to do with how traceable our origins are?

Sometimes I need both. My own mysterious strength of quantum genetics, of cape and revolution, of spin and stripe. Sometimes I need both to be strong and to be held. What if it is the world being the world that makes the sky the sky? What if the sky rushed in all directions to meet us here, connect us to everywhere? What if the ocean has my back? Could I trust that?

And who are you really, transatlantic Clymene? And what did you birth at the end of the world in the tempest of slavery off the side of the boat, what is your magic of spinning and cape, your consistent unheard of revolution of genes. Your journey accompanied and cloaked.

What did you find at the edge of yourself? Oh. Yes. Now I see it.

The sky.

What struck me first was this sentence: "Several of the captives have gained renown as quick learners and creative performers." They were talking about the oceanarium lives of the slope headed dolphins with the ridged teeth (*Steno bredanensis*), but I thought they were talking about you. And me. And all of our brilliant friends who have had to learn so fast, perform so creatively here in our captivity.

I kept reading. "At Sea Life Park in Hawaii, a Rough-toothed Dolphin mother and a Common Bottlenose Dolphin father produced a calf that lived for four years." The life span of this dolphin should be thirty-two years. What happened? I researched Sea Life Park, which celebrates its hybrids. They advertise on their website right now that you can swim with a "wholphin." Say they teach children about genetics with a special creature who is part bottlenose part false killer whale or was it melon headed whale, or was it…? 140 dolphins have died in captivity at Sea Life Park. The ones who are hybrids are marked as "UNSPECIFIED DOLPHIN OR PORPOISE" in all capital letters like that. Also none of their causes of death are listed definitively. But I dug and I dug as if morbidly compelled and I found the hybrid calf who lived four years. And according to this death record, she had no name but "HYBRID STENO MAMO" in all capital letters like that.

There is a 1974 article in the *Journal of Mammalogy* about this captive dolphin and her tragic story.[12] Her mother was born in the open ocean and captured in 1969, while pregnant. Shortly after arriving at Sea Life, newly captive she had a miscarriage. What did they name her? Makalani, the eye of

12 Thomas P. Dohl, Kenneth S. Norris, and Ingrid Kang, *Journal of Mammalogy* 55, No. 1 (February 1974): 217–22.

heaven. God is watching. At the time she became pregnant again, she was captive in a tank with two male bottlenose dolphins. The article does not characterize this as a breeding scheme, more like an aquatic housing crisis, but who knows. Three months before she gave birth, they placed her in a different tank with two female dolphins of her same species. She gave birth around 4pm on October 4, 1971. Scientists were allowed to come to the facility but not to measure the newborn or anyone else. If this dolphin lived, she would not only be a hybrid of two different dolphin species, but what scientists also had defined as two different dolphin families. A big deal. A small dolphin. Female, showing signs of both species, swimming clockwise around her mother perpetually. The other female dolphins with her helped the mother release her umbilical cord.

As a mother, Makalani was protective. Slapped a trainer who tried to move the young dolphin. Makalani attacked another person who tried to touch the baby. In Egypt, the name Makalani means "she knows." What did she know? The scientists looked on and referred to the newborn based on her talent for following her mother. They called her a "precocious youngster." When the scientists concluded their several months of observation they felt all signs were good. The dolphin was smart and well and protected. One day she would be a star performer at Sea Life Park. In their article, they proposed that maybe she was proof that those two different dolphin families weren't different families after all. What a victory for dolphin unity, conservation, education! This article is cited again and again in studies on dolphin hybridity.

But according to the death records this same precocious youngster died in 1975 at four years of age. Was Mamo her name? Her cause of death is left completely blank. The other causes of death at Sea Life are disturbing when listed: food poisoning, malnutrition, brain hemorrhages, multiple still births, killed by another dolphin. But they don't list the cause of death for this dolphin at all. What would be incriminating enough for this facility to refuse to mention? It leaves us to fabulation. The death records say Makalani died two years earlier. Was it the loss of her mother at two years old that did it? Did they separate the dolphins, try to breed the mother again? Were Makalani's actions against trainers in protection of her child too disruptive for the Sea Life way of living? Was it a housing problem, a feeding problem, an unanticipated function of being a dolphin that had never before existed in captivity?

Keiko Conservation, the organization that re-published the death records online, says that Sea Life Park should be shut down.[13] The Sea Life Park website says you can swim with dolphin hybrids and eat a meal with your family at an authentic nightly luau today if you want.[14] They don't say anything about a once famous hybrid who lived to be only four. They don't say anything about her mother who died four years after capture. Nothing on their website either about the dozens of spinner dolphins, bottlenoses, sea lions, seals who have died in their care over their forty-year existence. Some scientists, those who depend on dolphin and whale captivity for their research, protest the use of what they call biased terms like "emotional," "majestic," "children," "solitary confinement" in documents about marine mammals in captivity.[15] Because you might think of these animals as people— you know, as parents, as prisoners, as relatives, as friends.

Would that be wrong? I am related to all marine mammals. I am related to all those in captivity. I am writing this in honor of my great grandmother Edith who was not the only woman in our lineage to die captive in an asylum. They say she died of a broken heart after the death of her young son, my great-uncle, a disabled child who I never heard of until I found his name on an old census report and asked a

13 Https://www.keikoconservation.com/post/kamoana-s-death-marks -140-dolphins-that-have-died-in-sea-life-park-s-care.

14 Https://www.sealifeparkhawaii.com/.

15 Https://www.psychologytoday.com/us/blog/animal-emotions/201907 /orcas-are-majestic-emotional-beings-who-have-children.

question. He died in captivity too, after great grandma Edith succumbed to pressure from her community and especially my great grandfather (after whom little John Gibbs was named) to place him in an institution. He died there. In captivity. Within the first twenty-four hours. I have not heard the cause of his death in there.

Captives learn quick, perform creatively, or else. I am writing this for great grandmother Edith. The artist. Eye of heaven. In honor of what she knew even if she couldn't act on it. I am honoring her as who she is. Creator of the universe, source of all love. Thwarted protector of a child like no one had seen before. Her love never ended. Her love lives right now. Here in my breathing. I would swim around her clockwise. I would show her how her love survived all of this time, in the quick learning creatives who scream here in captivity. I am circling and circling her name. I am writing this for great uncle John Gibbs, the forgotten. The reclaimed. The proof that what they said family was, was not family. With a witness that it is not too late to create structures of care that honor his existence. To unlearn the hiding and the shame.

What I need to say is, you are. The walls around your life, the silence around your death, and the language all work to erase you and remove you from me, but they are not stronger than my grief, because my grief is fueled by love and I claim you. And I've come back for all the names I've never known since you were stolen. And I am never far away from you in fact. I am creator and creation. Right here, the source of all love ever. I strike away the lies about you with my lungs and tears, my circles and slaps. Eye of heaven. You are watching. And I don't know everything, but yet, I know.[16]

---

16 #nomorebackrooms #disabilityjusticenow #freeallmammals
#abolitionnow

Sometimes you will see an ocean dolphin in the river. One day standing on a dock in the Combahee River, looking for Harriet Tubman on the 149th anniversary of her successful uprising, my partner Sangodare and I saw three Atlantic bottlenose dolphins. Message received. A year later, we returned as twenty-one Black feminists to honor the 150th anniversary of the Combahee River raid together at the Mobile Homecoming project's Combahee Pilgrimage.

Decades earlier, my grandmother Lydia Gumbs got a message from some Atlantic bottlenose dolphins too, they inspired her design of the revolutionary flag, seal, and insignia of Anguilla: three bottlenose dolphins swimming in a circle. She colored the dolphins orange to represent endurance. The circle represented continuity. And though the revolution was short-lived, our listening continues. My sister has this symbol as a tattoo. It lives on as the major logo and symbol of Anguilla to this day.

And that day at the Combahee River I was wearing my grandmother's turquoise necklace. The sun was setting and the dolphins did indeed look orange as they swam in a circle under the Harriet Tubman Bridge and went back out to sea. Bottlenose message. Speaking across revolutions.

I wonder what it means for an ocean dolphin to swim up a river. The bottlenose has a range across the whole planet, the whole open ocean and yet sometimes they will choose the boundaries and specificity of a river, brackish water, narrow shores. Why?

The message for me today is about specificity. About choosing a lane with all my infinite potential. About how my world-traveling grandmother made a commitment to a small island. About how strong we grow sometimes, swimming upstream. About what the world can learn from the visibility of our message in a context that is specific enough to ring clear. And to trust that all water touches all water everywhere.

And for all of you, ocean dolphins, wondering "What am I doing in this river full of mud?" Remember why Harriet Tubman went south. She didn't have to. She was skilled, untraceable. She could have been individually free. Unencumbered. But if she wanted to tell an everlasting truth about freedom that would ring across the planet, a message for the ages, she had to live free in unfree space. It was the only way to bring us all with her.

Thank you, my loves, for the bravery of your freedom in spaces of clear limitation. In spaces of muddy reality. Thank you for your decisions to do not what you could do, but what you must. Thank you for teaching the difference between privilege and courage. Escape and transcendence. Reaction and revolution. Your endurance inscribes an eternal alternative, carried by bottles and bottlenoses, blood and breath. Message honored. Message received.

Sing the song of the new narluga or the old skull (my age) newly named. Sing the song of the twisted toothed of the bottom feeder of the thrice betrayed. Open mouth of the singing narluga whose song Sony Hifi did not record. Much is made of the narwhal mother who found in beluga whatever she found. Beluga is known for being whatever and changing forever into whatever's around. Knotted life of the noun narluga whose hybrid name means nothing much. Known only by the Indigenous hunter who kept the skull on his roof until taxonomists clutched. Wonder yet, at the penciled presumption of the shape one made in a break in the ice. Wonder yet at the warmth in the Arctic that makes life out of life against frigid advice. Call the name of the known narluga, which is not narluga and you do not know.

But imagine what it took without breakthrough technology to eat like a walrus but not haul onto ice. Or to gravitate towards pack ice and open water for the same reasons. Or to know yourself only by yourself and not from reflection anywhere nearby. Or to sing a song that means something, but only to you unless a nearby bowhead whale can remember something similar from centuries ago. Imagine what it is to be depicted in the newspaper based on an extrapolation of remains in the imaginations of the ones who hunt hunters. Or to know there are songs like "Baby Beluga" that are not about you. They are not about you. Or to sometimes, for a moment, know there has never been anyone more magical. Or to secretly inherit the powers of unicorns and shapeshifters in the bright cold dark of the 1980s. Or to die a thousand deaths of misrecognition, sacrificed to an insistence on the integrity of species. To remain impossible as long as species exist. Or to live forever for the same exact reason. And to sing.

four

practice

WHAT ARE THE INTERGENERATIONAL PRACTICES that gener-
ated dorsal fins in some dolphins and whales? What expe-
rience-based wisdom resulted in the ever-expanding spines
and blubber of bowhead whales or the adaptation of sideways
swimming river dolphins? What do the blue whales know
that lets them fast all day and sing across the planet?

I believe in the possibility of dorsal, or stabilizing practices in our own lives. I am committed to the development
of backbone and core muscle in the crooked life of at least
one person with scoliosis (me). We can cultivate practices
for finding each other in a shifting world. We can each create an intentional approach to what we take in and put out.
What are the intergenerational and evolutionary ways that
we become what we practice? How can we navigate oppres-
sive environments with core practices that build community,
resistance, and more loving ways of living?

Yes. I do have dorsal-fin envy. On the coast of North Carolina you can sometimes see the fins of *Lagenorhynchus actus* (*actus* means sharp) cutting through the water with clarity and grace. Who wouldn't want that?

The function of dorsal fins for aquatic animals is stability. In water that is always moving, having a dorsal fin provides balance, autonomy, and support for the swift turns you might have to make in this oceanic life. Yes. I need a dorsal fin to navigate all of this transformation.

How did dolphins get dorsal fins anyway? Unlike fish, they don't have bones that support a dorsal fin. The mammals they evolved through and from before returning to the ocean didn't have dorsal fins. They aren't a vestige of limbs like tail flukes and side fins may be. The prevailing explanation is that dolphins evolved the dense tissue that became dorsal fins because they needed to in order to live in the wild movement of the ocean. In other words, dolphins evolved dorsal fins from practice across generations. By accepting that the ocean would always move, and becoming accordingly. An embodied emphasis towards balance. That's what I'm talking about.

In a context that swells and tosses me around, where I might have to pivot without much warning, what are the evolutionary practices that stabilize me and allow me to cut a path through? This is one. Daily writing is my most dependable dorsal practice. It centers me, holds me, gives me perspective on what is changing in the ocean around me. It challenges me to notice my own drift. My daily writing, mirror and sound meditation, and Sharon Bridgforth's oceanic oracle decks extend my reach towards the ancestors at my back. Familiarize me with a love center I can return to any time. Another stabilizing force is the sound of my dear sister Yashna Maya Padamsee saying, "remember your breath" in the yoga videos that have been opening my shoulders for years. And my newest collective practice, Pilates with the divine Lana Garland is challenging me in ways I didn't know I needed. I am learning the language of the muscles that would allow me to move from my core. And when we exhale together in a downtown basement in Durham, we sound just like the recordings I listen to of dolphins surfacing and blowing out air.

Yes. I want a dorsal fin. I think I can make one if I practice.

What are your dorsal practices? What evolutionary repetitions have you cultivated to move through oceans? What are the ones you need to cultivate for the waves moving you now?

I am so grateful for the loving community of divine swimmers who have transformed my tissue by doing their work. I am grateful especially for my dispersed and displaced kindred, for teaching me to find stability in practice when, for our communities, housing and financial stability are often out of reach and capitalism tears our roots up again and again. Out here in the ocean we have our breathing and our practice. We have each other if we choose each other. *Lagenorhynchus actus*, also known as Atlantic white-sided dolphins, love to hang out with fin whales and humpbacks.

How did you do it? It's almost like you made something out of nothing, body where there was absence, but you didn't, you made life out of every day. You made it out of infinite love. Thank you for having my back. It still reaches for you. I love you for your breath, your dense, your stubborn growth impossible. Your evolution happening right now.[17]

---

17 You can see Yashna's throwback yoga classics that have been part of my daily life for a decade here: https://vimeo.com/user3944994. You can learn more about Sharon's oracle work here: https://www.datblackmermaidmanlady.com/oracle-deck. You can listen to Lana sharing wisdom on Osunfunke Omisade Burney-Scott's podcast here: https://anchor.fm/decolonizingthecrone/episodes/Aperture-Leo-Season-e4spou/a-akek3a. And as always you can support Michaela Harrison who is in Bahia breathing with whales right here: https://www.gofundme.com/f/5gyczp-whalewhispering.

The bowhead whale lives for centuries and could potentially grow forever. Researchers say their spines don't set, so even at two hundred years of age they might still grow. Yesterday, through a dear friend, a complete stranger gifted me a whale vertebra that might be from the eternally possible spine of a bowhead whale.

What a heavy piece of oracle. Yes. Honor the bowhead whale whose large proportion of body fat keeps them warm enough in the Arctic to outlive the various weapons used to kill them over time. I have said it before, I will say it again, fat is a winning strategy. New research suggests that young bowhead whales may even take nutrients from their bones, to further grow their baleen (the food filters in their mouths) in order to be able to eat more krill, grow more fat, live more better. Evolutionary geniuses.

My own backbone has been teaching me something too. My pediatricians diagnosed me with scoliosis as a school-aged child, and we may never know if I was born this gorgeously crooked or if the early weight of heavy books caused a shift in how I would carry myself through this life. What we do know? The books certainly were heavy and I haven't yet put them down. And also I walk, sit, and move in the world in a way that overstretches part of me, compresses the other side. My spine shoulders the tense work of keeping me togeth-er, keeping me from falling over as I lean through hallways, doors, and other passages.

Some say that the descendants of survivors of the middle passage all have our own version of pelvic and spinal tilt, of makeshift movement, of putting our bodies back together to somehow carry what we should never have had to car-ry. Some say, at this point in capitalism, we are all bent by the shapes we live through, which are conducive not to life but something else. And the bowhead whales? They saw the boats. Heard those same repurposed boats who came to kill them for their successful blubber, the oil that lit the books of blood and slavery. Even now, it is the commercial pursuit of another form of oil that threatens the bowhead whales whose fat fueled the capitalist project. Bowhead whales have breathed through so much history and outlived it too.

What does it mean, what does it take to grow regardless? Just this year I am learning to retrain my core muscles in a way that gives my back a break from all the breaking it has been doing over decades, using a method developed by an asthmatic athlete named Joseph Pilates, translated by a Black feminist filmmaker named Lana Garland.

In September 2019, along with some folks with endometriosis or who walk with canes or who live with other chronic shapes of tilt and pain, sometimes as a result of trauma, I kayaked for a week. Not straight, but well. And I thought about how between each vertebra there is a story pinched and breathing. And I felt how far I really have to grow. And though I don't have the luxury of centuries, I do have reach. I do have all the ways you stretch me. I do have violence to outlive and ice to break and songs to sing. I do have so much fat to earn and love to offer. Wisdom even. In these bones.

Indus susu and Ganges susu (also known as the two subspecies of the South Asian river dolphin) often swim sideways. Was this always the case? Even in the nineteenth century, when these dolphins swam in large groups, when there were no barges in the rivers, when the water was less polluted? Or is this an adaptation for a time in which they are mostly alone, divided from each other by structures they do not control but must nevertheless navigate? Sometimes they spiral through the water like a drill. They often quickly change directions. And you can see them swimming sideways, one flipper stirring up the sediment to find what they need to feed themselves, echolocating all along.

What about you? Are you swimming sideways? Keeping one ear to the Earth, one to the sky? Are you re-evaluating what you thought progress meant? Are you questioning the directions of your lines? I am. Indus and Ganges susu echolocate all the time; they are functionally blind and their movements through the river are not about day or night or getting somewhere. Heads bobbing, clicking continuously, they are asking where am I now and now and now? Which is necessary in rivers thick with nets, where your body is prized as bait, and aphrodisiac, and scarce research commodity.

Where are you now and now and now? Navigating planetary and political retrogrades? Do you feel like the world is on its side? Sometimes I do too. And I wonder who decided up and down? And what was I missing when I looked at the world top and bottom like they said? And what do I know about the world? It turns. I turn to you, disoriented. Where are we now?

In some areas, blue whales fast during the day. They eat in the evening and early in the morning. Think of that, the largest animal on the planet, whose stomach holds 2,200 pounds of food, just eating intentionally on the edges of the day. I like to think that we are all living in the long water prayer of the blue whales, that meditative sound that travels hundreds of miles underwater. With one breath they send sound across entire oceans, envelop the planet in far-reaching chant.

M. Nourbese Philip taught me that water holds sound, that it can reverberate on and on and keep on calling us. And so maybe the calls of the great blue whales who filled the whole ocean (before twentieth-century commercial ventures killed 95 percent of them) are still blessing our water selves now. Are still in residence, as Christina Sharpe reminds us. Right now, it is dangerous somehow to be visible in meditation and prayer. Yes. Imagine with me that the biggest sound on the planet, exceeding the anxiety we project over airwaves, is the prayer of blue ancestor depth. What then?

I honor the bravery of everyone fasting. The way you hold multitudes in your all-day-long prayer. And to all of us who could be more intentional about when, how, and what we transmit, about when, how, and what we take in, I send love.

five

collaborate

WHAT DOES IT MEAN TO function as a group in a changing environment? How can we organize ourselves intentionally to combat the imbedded isolation of late capitalism? It seems like the dolphins (and our other interloping sharks...the manta rays) have something to tell us. From mothering as an emergent strategy in massive dolphin super-pods to pantropical synchronized swimming as a model of being prepared for large-scale direct action, the dolphins are educating us on how to squad, or pod up.

Are we ready for a dolphin-informed replacement of the patriarchal family with "schools" of unlearning? What is the relationship between the circular collective feeding practices of manta rays and the Black diasporic history of cooperatives? I believe collaboration is natural and can be reclaimed.

Out here in the open ocean, mothering is an emergent strategy. Consider the white-bellied/short-snouted dolphins (*Lagenodelphis hosei*), who travel in groups of hundreds, sometimes thousands (Lesson 1: roll deep) and welcome several "other species" of dolphins and whales to swim and eat in community (Lesson 2: better together). Though they swim across the entire planet, no scientists (or no one willing to tell a western scientist) saw one alive until 1971. In fact, it seems there was a coordinated movement to be recognized because there were several different "first sightings" of the species on different parts of the planet…all somehow in 1971 (Lesson 3: we can be seen on our own terms)! The only requirements to be part of this massive oceanic family are that you gotta be willing to dive deep, because they eat a thousand feet below the surface (Lesson 4: do your depth work), and flock because they collectively change direction abruptly to keep humans from following them, and also move thousands of miles to stay current with the ocean (Lesson 5: be ready to transform).

Gratitude to my oceans of love, my expansive family in all directions. My mothers of all genders and ages and times. Thank you for nurturing me and holding me accountable in more ways than I can name.

Pantropical spotted dolphins are synchronized swimmers and community builders. They travel in pods of hundreds, but within the pods they organize into groups of twenty or less and time their diving and beautiful acrobatics to be exactly in sync. Out in the ocean, they participate in mobile interspecies collectives consisting of other dolphins (especially spinner dolphins), yellowfin tuna, and seabirds. Scientists have different theories about why they do this, most of which can be summarized in these words:

Knowing who they're with helps them know where they're at and where they want to be.

Maybe this is part of their pantropical resilience. Because, despite the serious and wasteful harm of decades of tuna-net strangulation, they remain one of the most abundant species of dolphin on the planet. I think of those great organizers with pantropical visions (Claudia Jones, Shirley Chisolm, Mila Aguilar, Mama Tingo… Hallelujah, there are too many to name). I also think, of course, of the Subversive Sirens, a gold-medal-winning, synchronized-swimming team based in the Twin Cities who are committed to Black liberation, queer visibility, and body positivity. I think about the Ready the Ground Training Team in the North Carolina Triangle area where I live, making direct action possible and graceful and safe.

And as always I think about you. When I can't see the shore I'm here timing my breathing to yours. Knowing collectively we can leap, we can dive, we can practice our faith in each other. Remembering, as Toni Cade Bambara says, "the seabirds are still alive."[18]

From the sky, a dolphin pod of *Lissodelphis* (Black and white dolphins with no fins), which travel by the hundreds (up to three thousand strong) would look like a smooth Black continent of movement. From underwater, it would look like a white cloud that somehow submerged. That's how I imagine it. Collectively echolocating for food, they would be impossible to ignore. Though only a few come to the surface at a time, they travel by the hundreds or thousands. So sleek. And

18 Toni Cade Bambara, *The Seabirds Are Still Alive* (New York: Random House, 1977).

their cousins—other dolphins with fins (not so smooth)—
they welcome them into the pod too.

That's how I think about us sometimes. Those of us who
have chosen to move together through this. We are perceived
so distinctly from different directions. Human observers mistake *Lissodelphis* for seals or sea lions, or even for penguins
sometimes. Which is to say, maybe it's not so much about
being recognized as who we are as it is about staying together, feeding each other, knowing where we are, and moving through.

My love to my pod in all directions. The smooth and the
not quite so smooth. Those of you showing your back and
those showing your belly. Those of you breaking through the
surface and those staying in the deep. It's an honor to be in
the midst of you. Look around, listen out. Here we are.

If a school of *Lissodelphis* don't want you to see them, you
won't. They will time their movements to the waves, they will
breathe at the rate of the ocean herself. As above, so below.
From the sky, they will look like the ocean, from the ocean
they will look like the sky.

And they stay in a tight formation. So they can move
undetected.

There is one species of *Lissodelphis* in the northern hemi-
sphere and one in the south. As above, so below. The guidebooks say there is no overlap in range, which means they
never see each other. But I wonder. I wonder about the planet
itself as a mirror. A sphere of parallel existence. Am I not par-
ticipating in a dance with those beyond where I can touch,
or know, or swim to? In my breathing, I am balancing the
seen and the unseen, learning to cultivate a graceful way to
be both ocean and sky.

I am studying how to be in school with you. I time my breathing to your heart to find the ocean. My heart will race to meet your laughter: you are sky.

As below, so above.

Choreographic presence, circumpolar hold, deep listening, coordination. Call back the school that fear untaught me. Give me the heartbeat I remember. Call it love.

The primary unit of life for striped dolphins (*Stenella coeruleoalba*) is school. The nurturing of the children happens in schools of between twenty-five and seventy-five dolphins. And school also continues. Schools of adults. Schools of juveniles. School is necessary.

For example, in the early 1990s, when a disease outbreak in the Mediterranean Sea decreased the school sizes of the surviving dolphins to about seven, they reorganized themselves, found each other, and kept having school at the size that was optimal to them.

I know that what scientists mean when they call groups of dolphins "schools" is not exactly what I usually mean when I, Black feminist book nerd say "school," but these dolphin schools are organizational structures for learning, nurturance, and survival, both intergenerationally and within generations. I think about how my grandfather used to say *school* (like the secret name of the true god, the most necessary possible thing) and how much faith he put in the idea of school, which sometimes meant investing in educational institutions that may not have deserved all that faith.

What if school, as we used it on a daily basis, signaled not the name of a process or institution through which we could be indoctrinated, not a structure through which social capital was grasped and policed, but something more organic, like a scale of care. What if school was the scale at which we could care for each other and move together. In my view, at this moment in history, that is really what we need to learn most urgently.

Legally and narratively, our society encourages small, isolated family units and an anti-social state reluctant to care. So care becomes the unsustainable work, the massive unpaid labor that breaks backs, hearts, and the visionary will of multitudes on a regular basis. (More on this in Leah Lakshmi Piepzna-Samarasinha's *Care Work*.)[19] What can we learn about the failure of the imagined ideal household? What could we learn if we cared to learn?

In a striped dolphin school, only up to one-third of the school is visible at the surface. What scale and trust would it take to rotate our roles, to work not to fulfill a gendered lifetime ideal (husbandwifemotherfatherdaughterson) but to show up and sink back, knowing there is enough of all the forms of nurturance to go around in cycles? Striped dolphin schools don't bother with shallow water, they go deep off the continental shelf. What would it mean to go deep with each other? What are the scales of intimacy and the actual practices that would teach us how to care for each other beyond obligation or imaginary duties. Striped dolphins eat fish with luminous organs that live in the deep scattering layer of the sea. What nourishes them is literally what lights them up inside! Could we be like that?

I am wondering if we could trade the image of "family" for the practice of school, a unit of care where we are learning and re-learning how to honor each other, how to go deep, how to take turns, how to find nourishing light again and again.

And love to the ways you already reach out and resist how the tax code and the work week and the subdivision want us not to learn to do this. And remember that Grace

---

19 Leah Lakshmi Piepzna-Samarasinha, *Care Work: Dreaming Disability Justice* (Vancouver: Arsenal Pulp Press, 2018).

Lee Boggs said if we could work intergenerationally as solutionaries to all the challenges to our wellbeing and existence that would be all the school we would need?[20] We would learn everything right there. I do not commit to playing a permanent role in a structure designed for our infinite lack. But I do commit to playing with you. I think we have already learned that what the movies say family is, is not a sustainable scale. And in trying to force it, to *perform it* we suffer so much.

We are struggling because, over and over again, we feel like we are not good enough family members, but what if we just need to go back school? Meaning, what if there is no such thing as "good enough" in a structure too small for the necessary adaptations of life? What if all those ways we feel like failures in our families are not failures at all, but a pre-school lesson that could teach us to restructure our care?

What I do commit to for this lifetime and as many as I get, is to learn with you always. To study the changes you bring to my body, my spirit, my mind. To be in school with you for the duration, in a curriculum called "how we endure." I do commit to rigorously learning how to gracefully collaborate, and step back when it's your turn with nothing to prove. I do commit to the work of going deep enough to find the necessary food that lights us up inside. I love you, and I have so much to learn. I love you and we are just now learning that it's possible, love on a scale we can survive. I love you, and how generous—how downright miraculous—it is that life would let me learn like this.

20 Grace Lee Boggs, Opening Ceremony at the Allied Media Conference in Detroit Michigan, 2007.

The northern limit of the range of the white-beaked dolphin crosses into the edge of the Arctic. But they have not adapted to ice. That means that water itself can become a threat, freezing them out of their feeding grounds, surrounding them and trapping them with no nearby access to food, at worst suffocating them under what seems like a sudden white weight. Gradually they can't live where they lived. Sometimes they are forced to beach themselves into even less survivable situations.

Do you know something about this? Any of us still not adapted to how cold capitalism is? Do you know something about this Durham, Detroit, Oakland? About what it feels like to be iced out (did she say *priced out*?) of the habitat you made intriguing over soul generations? The cost of cool.

At the same time, the rising temperatures of the ocean are negatively impacting the food supply of these dolphins across their range too. Too hot to handle, too cold to hold. (Quoth the man who was iced out of New Edition.)[21]

What do you do when where you live becomes inhospitable to your living? White-beaked dolphins collectivize. (By the way, their beaks aren't even necessarily white—these dolphins are mostly Black, but we know something about emphasizing white potential over Black presence by now, right?) They collectively forage and congregate in the hundreds or thousands. Maybe they know what community land trusts know: You can't effectively respond to gentrification with individual buying choices one household at a time; it takes a collective.

Remember when Ida B. Wells helped organize a mass exodus from Memphis? I'll remind you:

Here is Ida B. Wells in an editorial in her own newspaper: "The city of Memphis has demonstrated that neither character nor standing avails the Negro if he dares to protect himself against the white man or become his rival, the city will

---

21 Bobby Brown. "On Our Own," *Ghostbusters 2 Soundtrack*, MCA Records, 1989.

neither protect our lives and property, nor give us a fair trial in the courts, but takes us out and murders us in cold blood." (This was 1892. But does it sound familiar?) According to *The Selected Works of Ida B. Wells-Barnett*: "For nearly three months, Black people left Memphis 'by the scores and hundreds,' supported financially by Wells and others who remained in town. This continued until the white citizenry, feeling the loss of manual labor and business income, appealed to Wells to halt the exodus. She refused."[22]

Dolphins know how to travel in masses too. I wonder if responding to violent strictures on human migration and systemic displacement of communities of color also requires collaboration beyond species. These dolphins travel with other dolphins and with fin and humpback whales in huge groups conducive to safety and collaboration. What interspecies collaborations (and I'm not talking about dog parks) do we need in this time of freezing melting adaptation?

And what could I tell you that would help you remember how necessary you are in the time of disposability?

How about this:

The world wants to be wherever you are. They get there with the tools they have. Turns out, the tools are weapons. But the universe has a Black technology. It is massive. It is body temperature. It is the space between us, rich with stars, renewable and irreplaceable at the same time. Maybe the world can exist without you in it. But I cannot. There is no such thing as home unless I'm with you. No such thing as home unless you're here.

22 Ida B. Wells, *The Selected Works of Ida B. Wells-Barnett*, compiled and with an introduction by Trudier Harris-Lopez (Oxford: Oxford University Press, 1991), 6.

The manta ray, unlike other stingrays, doesn't actually have anything to sting you with. Unlike other sharks or their shell-breaking ray cousins, close cartilage relatives, they don't have sharp teeth. They are filter feeders. They are breathing plankton. Sometimes cooperatively. What they are practicing is a time-compressed version of "partner," as we would call it in Jamaica, or as our other Caribbean and West African cousins might say "susu." They gather in a circle and flap their watery wings to collect as much plankton as possible and take turns eating while the rest of the circle holds the space.

I recognize you, not of sharpened teeth or stinging tail, yet wide of wing, embracing salt, shaping nutrition with your mouth at the center of your chest. I would love it if I could be so coordinated as to keep my mouth closed while dancing resources towards you, your open heart. It might also help if I could filter what I need from everything else floating around me.

So, yes. I can commit to open arms, vulnerable face, to staying in the circle with you, patient in the practice. And what had been my sharp becomes my specificity, and what had been my barbs become my wings.

be vulnerable

I WONDER WHAT OUR SENSITIVE edges have to teach us. What do our mortality and openness mean to the ecology we could surrender to together? In this section, I explore my own strange teeth, our tendency to hurt people who have already been hurt in similar ways to us, and what it takes to actually lead on the issues that have impacted us the most. Marine mammals live in a volatile substance whose temperature is changing for reasons not of their own making. Their skin is always exposed, they are surrounded on all sides by depth. What could enable us to live more porously, more mindful of the infinite changeability of our context, more open to each other and to our own needs?

Pacific white-sided dolphins (sometimes called "lags") are social animals. They congregate with many other species of whales, dolphins, and porpoises—even seals, sea lions, and sea birds for that matter. They practice collaborative foraging and fishing. They sometimes travel in schools of thousands, or hundreds, or tens.

Within these groups though, observers have noticed a pattern. What the guidebooks call "close knit" groups of five or less dolphins within a school who seem to have made a "lasting alliance" with each other. What marks these cliques within the pod?

Actual marks. They are "heavily scarred."

Whence these scars? Are these particular dolphins survivors of attacks by orca, a known predator to this species? Are they survivors of tuna nets or fishing boat propellers? Or did they scar each other? Some scientists think these may all be male dolphins. Have they fought each other and nonetheless decided to be best friends? Maybe they are simply elders who have been hurt by all of the things I mentioned and yet are wise enough to keep each other close.

I wonder why sometimes we congregate with those who have been hurt in ways that look similar to how we have been hurt. About how we sometimes (me too) name identities and even whole organizations based on our scars. And how sometimes those of us with similar vulnerabilities are the ones who scar each other. I wonder sometimes about what keeps us close, in a hurting world shaped by intimate violence. In a world that cuts systemically and deep.

Another thing. The scars on dolphins and whales also tell their would-be benefactors who they are. It is how observing scientists tell them apart. It is useful for getting an accurate count, for tracking behavior across expeditions. A dolphin with scars is more likely to be known, recognized, named by the watchers. Mentioned in funding reports.

Do I do that too? Are my wounds the most convenient ways for you to know me? Why do they shape so much of how I know myself? And the whole dynamic of recognition, how does it shape and scar us?

What I know is that I was not wrong when I chose to hold you close and stay in range. I knew. I always knew we were still healing. And you could see right away that I was not perfect. You could see some piece of what the world had done. And yet, what has been done, though still not over, is not the end. And your scars are not all I know about you. And my scars are not all I want you to know. And your name is made where life makes itself in me. And your name is medicine over my skin. And our kinship is the kind of salve that heals whole oceans. And love is where I know and do not know you. And love is where we began and where we begin.[23]

The story of how *Stenella attenuata* did not get her spots back.[24] Or how she hid. Or why, unlike Pantropical spotted dolphins elsewhere, do Pantropical spotted dolphins in the Atlantic (not to be confused with Atlantic spotted dolphins in the Atlantic) appear not to have spots?

She hid. The best way to not be spotted (in the descriptive infinitive) is to not be spotted (in the sense of the passive tense), or vice versa. Because once they spot you that's it. So she hid. That's one way to say it.

Another way to say it is that in the warm Atlantic anything is possible. And even the strongest swimmer must reckon with the attenuations of the bloodwashed Atlantic, the site of a sea change in the meaning of skin. A need for stealth.

23 #junejordan #soldier #civilwars #dryvictories

   Direct quotes: *National Audubon Society Guide to Marine Mammals of the World.*

24 This is a reference to *How Stella Got Her Groove Back*, the film (1998) and book (New York: Signet, 1996) by Terri McMillan.

What do I know about this? I know about hiding. I know about creating an opaque image unattenuated by grief, insecurity, and shame. At least I think I do. Many times I have showed up and allowed you think I am here by myself. Not attended by ghosts. Not haunted by everything. The best way not to be spotted is not to be.

But what if something else is possible, and my sweat is at stake. What if the repression of my freckled faults and fears is exactly what will stop me from honoring the ocean of my love, which is older than slavery and lived millennia without shame. What if my swimming unseen sacrifices the wisdom that would waken within you if you saw? What if I've trained you to ignore the truth about me at your peril and mine? What then?

There are many dolphins in the genus *Stenella*, striped and spotted, spinners and the hybrid clymene. What if we are all necessary in our specificity? Can I trust you to love me with spots? If you clock me, is the time up?

I do know that sometimes people have seen a part of themselves in me too messy to bear. Do I cherish my wildness more than I fear their rejection? Sometimes if I feel all my emotions in public I can't make myself speak. But sometimes I speak anyway. And my first marine mammal lesson was that if I breathe I can still speak even while crying. I can breathe through salt water. I can live through this mess.

Mammal recognize mammal. More recognize more. I love you and your spots and the spot we are in for all that it is teaching us. I love you and your skin, as the meaning of skin meets its most strenuous test. I love everything you hid and everything you gave and everything you showed and everything you made while you waited for me to notice. And the ocean is wide through my every pore. Salt recognize salt. More recognize more.

Walrus tusks never stop growing. The sign of an elder walrus who has evaded the ivory economy is what we call being long in tooth. And indeed the long front teeth of the walrus lead them in their movements. First sense the ice in front of them. Leverage their whole weight as they transition between depth and surface.

National Geographic translates the scientific name of the walrus (*Odobenus rosmarus*) as "tooth-walking sea horse." Could I evolve to walk with my teeth?

By the way, my teeth have very deep roots. Almost none of my baby teeth fell out. Ever. Except for one or two, they all had to be extracted. As an adult I found out I had six wisdom teeth that were then extracted too. Looking at the x-rays I started to think maybe I was an evolutionary throwback. My very own ancestor. Sometimes I miss all those teeth. And my overbite. So much has happened with these bones in my head. Such reshaping of my prehistoric mouth. What have I forgotten? Do you know that even after surgery, years later, a rooted piece the oral surgeons missed still offered up another tooth? Persistent, these ancestors in my mouth. And I give thanks.

Sometimes I wish I lived in a world where teeth were never for sale (to fairies or anyone else), where smiles were not commodified, where showing my teeth was something I never forced myself to do. That I could be as long in action as I am in talk. That where my mouth led was somewhere the whole weight of me could follow. Is it? Can I?

We do often lead with the feelings we can't ignore. From toothache, from trigger, from nerve. And what if, with every bark or bite, we thought about the blubbered tons behind our every movement. What it actually takes to move into the sun.

And how I love you. With the sensitivity you cannot hide. With words you can't take back. With teeth that cannot fit in a closed mouth. With faith that cannot help but lift you somewhere. You learned to trust the growing part of you to lead you home. You did. You do it daily. So brave. And strong. Your forward face. Your growing bones. Your wisdom.

be present

HERE WE ARE, WHERE PRESENCE meets offering, looking to Indus river dolphins who live by constantly using sound to mark where they are, spinner and beneguela dolphins who do somersaults for no scientifically agreed-upon reason. What could it mean to be present with each other across time and space and difference? Presence is interpersonal and interspecies and intergalactic, in some ways eternal. How can we rethink our presence on the planet and its precarity by paying attention to how the Indus dolphins have brought themselves back from the brink of extinction? Could we learn to love the humpback whale beyond its marketable mythology and love ourselves beyond what capitalism tells us is valuable about being us? Marine mammal mentorship offers us the chance for presence as celebration, as survival and its excess, as more than we even know how to love about ourselves and each other.

Most cetaceans have a crystalline lens over their eyes so they can see underwater. The South Asian river dolphins do not. Also the water moves so quickly, and is so full and turbid that not much would be visible if they were looking with their eyes. So they look instead with their voices.

The Indus and Ganges river dolphins live in sound. They make sound constantly, echolocating day and night. In a quickly moving environment they ask where, again where, again where.

The poem of the Indus river dolphin is the ongoing sound of here, a sonic consciousness of what surrounds them, a form of reflective presence. Here.

The home of the Indus river dolphin has gone through many manmade changes. First of all, pollution. First of all, illegal poverty-induced fishing methods. First of all, before that, a legend about a sea monster, and more recently, in the 1980s, a takeover of the river banks of Sindh by the Daku Raj, a group of organized gangs who effectively scared all the fisherfolk away. Through all of it, the Indus river dolphin, who clicks all day and night, has been saying, here. Here. Here. Here. In a language I want to learn. According to the scientists who have been counting the endangered Indus river dolphin population since 1972, their population has steadily increased every year. From 132 when they first started count-ing to 1,419 this year. Here. Here. Here.

In the language I was raised in, "here" means "this place where we are," and it also means "here" as in "I give this to you." Could I learn from the Indus river dolphin a language of continuous presence and offering? A language that brings a species back from the brink, a life-giving language? Could I learn that? Could we learn that? We who click a different way, on linked computers day and night?

What I want to say to you requires a more nuanced field of receptive language than I have ever spoken. It requires me to reshape my forehead, my lungs. It requires me to redis-tribute my dependence on visual information. So I will close my eyes and say it: Here. Here I am. Here I am with you.

Here is all of me. And here we are. Here. Inside this blinding presence. Here. A constant call in a moving world. Here. All of it. Here. Here. Humbly listening towards home. And here. And here. Right here. My poem for you. My offered presence. This turbid life. Yes. Here you go.

And then there are the ones who just show off. "Spinner" is the name given to a variety of dolphins all over the world who spin around themselves three to seven times in one leap and then land in the water again. There are a number of theories as to why they would do this, but no one really knows. Maybe we're missing the message.

But then, if you could fly, windmill around yourself rotating like a planet on a planet in a sea pulled by a moon, wouldn't you? With pods up to three thousand and a beautifully promiscuous practice of anytime birth and all-day mating and many parents, the definition of family for spinner dolphins seems to be: whoever's here. And even the scientists are catching it. Because the definition of a spinner dolphin seems to be "whoever spins like that." (There are many different populations of different sizes, appearances, geographies, and behaviors all grouped under the name.)

And I too seem to know you, not by where you live or what you eat, but by what you do for no known reason. Or a reason so obvious there is no need to explain. I would love to let go of the spinning of the capitalist wheels in my mind and meet the air on all my sides. If I could fly, surrounded all around by other dancers, chosen kin, free without an underbelly hid. I would. I did, it seems. Some time ago. Remember? You were there.

Pretty good chance that today there are some handsome dolphins off the coast of Namibia doing somersaults.

The benegeula dolphin teaches of cycles. For example, maybe some of the ancestors of these dolphins were flipping out when, in 1982 (the year of my birth), Alexis De Veaux (first of our name) was in NYC listening for news of a free Namibia and not getting that news. In the pages of *Essence Magazine*, Alexis said: "Well I cannot look in the mirror and not see Namibia."[25] Cannot look and not see. She called on Black women in the US to relate to the struggle of SWAPO (the South West African People's Organization) as a lesson on the complexity of liberation in our own lives. Like that move where you leap out of your situation, arch your body fantastically, then splash down where you were, more aware of your roundness.

Alexis De Veaux teaches of reflection and Black feminist solidarity. Of how the self is not an individual unit for success within the system that exists, but a collective Black interface seeking something else. Listening darkly. It is an invitation to find in each "other" exactly what we are afraid of finding in our "selves." And of course, I cannot look at Alexis and not see Alexis. So I study Alexis.

Beneguela dolphins (in our household we call them handsome Namibian dolphins) don't do somersaults in isolation to impress themselves. They leap and make circles strictly during social interaction. When I am with you, I remember this was never a straight line. I remember how movement is round. And this is why I celebrate. This is why I listen for you with the urgency and consistency of morning. Because your

25 Alexis De Veaux, "Listening for the News," *Essence Magazine,* March 1982.

love is an ocean recurring. Your love is my face meeting sky. Let me give you every angle of me. Here, watch this!

Praise the humpback whales' PR person for making cetaceans relatable to the landed inhumane. The singing breaching whale on most of the posters. How did the humpback become the most studied whale? One thing that helps, when those who are studying you are capitalists, is that humpback whales are easy to identify as individuals because of the markings on their tails. And the story is that humpback whales are pretty solitary creatures, except for at mating time, and even then they meet in small groups.

Two years ago, however, off the coast of South Africa, an unprecedented (as far as you know) gathering of hundreds of young humpback whales stumped scientists. What were they doing? And just last week a strange, skinny, seemingly sickly humpback whale swam into the San Francisco Bay and got a nickname. "Allie." Mmhmm.

And what I wonder is, what happens when we shift our behavior beyond the characteristics most palatable to predatory "allies"? What happens when we value our mass impact as much as or more than our unique and haunting songs? And after we finish proving we are smart and capable of feeling to those who somehow think that it is wise to boil the world, what then?

I love the parts of you that no one thinks are particularly special. I love the basic you of you unmarketable and everyday. I love to be around you because the round around you thrills me. And let's get together again soon. A whole bunch of us. I love you more than press conferences can say. Breach when you want to.

eight

be fierce

DID YOU HEAR ABOUT THE rainbow-breathing whale that straight up swallowed a white South African diver? Marine mammals live with a graceful ferocity, navigating treacherous circumstances daily. What can we learn from the orca, for example, about the sad farce of human dominion? Or from dolphins that demand fish from the humans who impinge on their food supply? Or from the leopard seal who is so fierce I dare compare her to the incisive Toni Morrison (not a comparison I would ever make lightly)? What is our bravest breathing? What is our unapologetic action towards self-determination?

If you let them tell it, before 1970, the orca, codename Blackfish, were despised. Military bases had guns pointed towards the water to kill them on sight for no nourishing reason. Teenage boys shot them with 22s and slashed them with knives and left them to die slow, painful deaths, and the adults in their communities applauded them for taking down a giant pest.

What about post-1970, with the capture of Namu and a whole generation of Southern resident orcas, mostly babies? If you let them tell it, thanks to oceanarium marketing, orcas are "loved"—meaning featured on posters, made into stuffed animals, starring as the main attractions at Sea World. Marketable captives for capitalism. "Loved."

I advocate for a different definition. I would say the orca before and after 1970 are influential. In matrilineal, multi-generational groups all over the planet, orca families influence all the other species in their range. They inspire seals to move onto land, they impact the migration of animals as varied as moose and humpback whales. In truth, the orca is a large dolphin, but there is no species on Earth too large to fear her. And give respect. Orcas greet each other respectfully as distinct resident groups and celebrate their own social order. They collaborate on the care of their young. They are not afraid to express their grief for months and years in public. Yes, I would say the orcas are powerful, influential, necessary. Nuanced and majestic, brave and committed. Those are the words I would use.

So whereas the Miami Seaquarium says that an orca named "Lolita" is a beloved attraction for all ages, and is safer in the smallest cell to ever hold an orca than she would be in her resident home in the Salish Sea, I add my voice to the voices of her Lummi relatives and say, that's not her name. And it never was. This summer the Lummi had a naming ceremony for this whale, who is sometimes known as Tokitae. Her new and sacred name is Sk'aliCh'elh-tenaut, a name that refers to a native village near the range in which she would live if she had never been captured; a group of people with whom she could have been in tangible sacred relationship; a name, which as I read it, means home. The possibility of home for the last surviving member of her generation, who were captured by scores for the "love" of orca fandom.

What does it actually mean to love someone whose love leads generations? Ecosystems shape themselves around her. Great and small dream her at night. What does it mean to love someone who has seen her children taken, and, at the risk of capture, stayed to witness and scream? Who will carry around the corpse of her child until her grief has reached another stage? Who will not pretend that her heart is not broken when it is? Do we know how to love a love that huge and unapologetic? Could we learn that?

I am grateful for the Lummi who are currently suing for repatriation. I support their just demand that Sk'aliCh'elh-tenaut be returned to her home, which is her name, return her to her name, which is her home. Can you not hear that? Her name is Home. She should be there inside her name.

I love you with a love of screams. I love you with a love of witness. I love you with a love so old and deep, so complicated I can't name it. Oh love, if I could live inside my name. I say it, love. I want to live there, in a home where home is home. I live a love you cannot grasp or capture. I want to live inside my name. My name is love. I want to live in love as home, I want to live in it. Expansive and influential. Specific and sacred. I want to earn the right to say it to you. Love.

Scientists say that Indo-Pacific bottlenose dolphins are "relatively aggressive."[26] They reclaim fish from the lines and nets of commercial and sport fishers who are draining their food

---

26 Smithsonian's *Guide to Marine Mammals of the World.*

supply. In Shark Bay, Australia, they started vocally demanding a tax (in the form of fish) from fishing boats in the 1960s. And it was offered. Now tourists in that bay gladly bring the offering for the pleasure of being screamed at by a dolphin who then snatches a fish from your hand. (We all have our interspecies role-play dreams, I guess.)

I am proud of you dolphins who live among sharks, like the Indo-Pacific bottlenose does in much of her range. Thank you for the sharp messages writ in your scars. The bite marks you wear as you demand back your birthright. Sharks usually try to eat Indo-Pacific bottlenose dolphins at a very young age. So the dolphins stay close to each other and loud. And they gang up on fishing boats demanding their due.

I am first of all grateful that you have survived to yet shout one more day in the face of all theft. I'm in awe of how you look power right in the eye with the gall of what you know, need, and remember. I know our reparations will come from your leadership. Your wounds and their wisdom. Your knowledge of teeth. Your brave associations. Do you hear me here screaming beside you? Stay close.

The leopard seal is not afraid of you. She is not afraid of you. She never was. She remains a mystery to you. You would have to study her on her own terms and you don't know how yet. It's okay. You can admit you've been afraid of how she knows exactly who she is. Her haunting song. All around Antarctica on pack ice and in water, she is in charge. If you come to hunt her, she will hunt you better, because she's at home.

Black and white? That's a snack to her. A penguin or a random platypus, it all nourishes something deeper sleeker, older. Blacker than the Black of Blackandwhite can handle, truth be told. She is indeed too cold to hold. Not yours to grasp.[27]

For all these reasons the leopard seal can afford to be generous. She can give you everything you don't deserve. Though you may not see it as generosity at first. She will pop your inflatable boat so you can know it was only air. What you think keeps you afloat does not support you. She will show you how it feels to be hunted, an opportunity if you can take it, to unlearn your predatory presumptions.

Photographer Paul Nicklen says she once brought him random penguins, again and again.[28] What do you think? Eleven times? Lined them up so you could see the writing on the ice. Look what I found, now take the picture. Yes, she will teach you something if you let her.

How did she do it? How did she make the bottom of the planet the apex? How did she make the whole Black and white bird without wings seem so small in the depth of the ocean? How did she sing out from under water and ice a song so haunting it can never be forgotten?

All I know is I am grateful for how wide you opened your mouth, for the oceans you let through you, for your fierce and knowing movement. All your regal reckoning. They say your name means "I work water, slender claw." And yes. I say every scratch is script and scripture. I say, like water, you shape stone and land and history. Author of worlds, you give us more than we can earn.

---

27 #restinpowertonimorrison

28 Ron Leach, "Nat Geo Photographer Comes Face to Face with Massive Leopard Seal in Antarctica," *Shutterbug*, April 21, 2016. https://www.shutterbug.com/content/national-geographic-photographer-comes-face—face-massive-leopard-seal-antarctica-video.

They call him the Weddell seal, but that is not his name. No mammal lives as far south as he does, except sometimes you. He dives deep under the ice and sings. And when you wake up in the middle of the night and the ice is shaking with sounds like 80s movies about aliens, that's him reminding you who he is.

Scientists make their own fiction. They say that the sound is about mating, but he doesn't even mate until his life is half over. They say it must be about territory. But there is no one here but you. And us. Spread out across the whole bottom of Earth.

And he will dive 2,600 feet down and use the Earth itself, a magnetic field of resonance, to find the one small hole he made to breathe. Do you not hear that? And you think he's not tracking you back, tracker? Listen. Just listen. He heats the air around him as he breathes it. What do you think they call him where he's from? You say his mouth curved up with broken teeth looks like he's smiling at you. And why? When Weddell was a murderer who came to kill his ancestors, which means you are calling him out of his name. Smile at you? When you now say he is abundant enough to kill "experimentally" while you melt the entire place he lives. You live here too.

And if you knew what it took for him to come back from the brink of extinction you would not be living in the science fiction you create and fund with death. Listen closely to the sound of frozen breath. He's smiling.

I know why he's smiling. Because you amuse us. You hear a spaceship and keep looking up. We're here already.

All my love to the spaceships on and under ice. Your movements guided by what no one else can see. Your voice a sound that no one could expect to hear, except we do. Thank you for your out of this world presence. Thank you for trusting what you feel and coming back. Your heartbeat a portal below everything else on Earth. Your smile, hint of a depth I don't deserve yet. And love can make me alien and new. And humble on a planet I don't know, although I live here. And gentle with the galaxies within me screaming home.

Apparently the Black-chinned dolphin in Tierra del Fuego and the southern coast of South America does not whistle, she thrashes. Sometimes *Lagenothynchus australis* is called an "entrance" animal because she lives in the swift moving water, the narrow spaces, the entrances to channels, the kelp forests, and estuaries. Maybe Audre Lorde would say she loves in doorways coming and going.[29]

Though they are one of the few dolphins that scientists believe never whistle, they must communicate somehow because they choreograph. Sometimes they stretch out into a line to feed cooperatively, or make a large circle. Or in their most impressive synchronized swimming move, they make a flower formation with their bodies and flail until they create their own whirlpool and everyone eats.

Yes. Sometimes you do have to make your own whirlpool, redirect the waters, initiate a spiral of momentum that can displace whole governments. And I respect that. Respect and love for those who thrive in narrow places, the in-between spaces of change. Gratitude to those who have made movement their method, upheaval their home. And who, without even a whistle, know when to get in line, when to make a circle, when to spin the ocean. And know it with the drum of their whole bodies. Who have so practiced merengue that they know just when to turn. Whose bomba call and response has become seismic now. Impossible to ignore.

And thank you for your grace, the way your necessary agility in the face of closed doors and narrow passages has made you that much more attuned to how we move together. And thank you for your willingness to churn the waters up. Alone

---

29 Audre Lorde, "A Litany for Survival," in *The Black Unicorn* (New York: W.W. Norton, 1978), 31.

you are an acrobat, the bravest of survivors. Together though, we show the ocean the edge of itself, show the tide the turn within us. Thrash a language out of action. Get fluent, loved ones. Watch our bodies. We speak change.[30]

You say beluga, I say shapeshifter. Is that the whale? No, it is just a piece of ice, a seabird in the distance, the whitecap of a wave itself. One experienced researcher gives this advice: look for a white spot that grows, shrinks, and disappears. Does some idea of whiteness keep them looking and not seeing? All they remember for sure is an undulating motion. Look for that, they say. Like they've been glamored. And bioacoustic researchers hear everything: the sound of a canary, an orchestra tuning up, a crowd of children shouting in the distance. Maybe the sailors were right when they called you mermaid, said they heard you sing them home.

What I know is that you are loud in cold places. Longed for whether you are here or not. Your cervical vertebrae are unfused so you can move your neck in all directions. And you, do. You can change the shape of your head and face by breathing. They say your lips are perfectly shaped to spit in the face of anyone watching. I think I know you. I know you gather by the thousands to all give birth together. You return again and again to the places your mothers visited while they held you. Sometimes you get stranded and yet survive until the next tide. Yes. Something about you feels familiar to me too.

My love to all the magic beings on the edge of imagination. How could they do anything but make up legends

30 #rickyrenuncia #wandarenuncia #puertoricoisaBlackgeography #throwthewholeadministrationout #oyaforpresident #allempiresfall #itsthe121anniversaryoftheUSinvasionofPR #justsayin

in the face of all of this? All this thick and agile movement, all this demonstrated love? And when you think you see and hear me, you actually just learn yourself. Let that be beautiful for you. And meanwhile remember to come back, give life and celebrate creation. That was love. It wasn't your imagination.

The tropical whale (*Balaenoptera edeni*) is now studied as not just a whale species, but as a whole whale complex. Two or three or maybe four species are now in the conversation. Thanks to molecular research in Aruba in 2012, the whales in the Caribbean Sea are thought to be in a clade with whales on the coast of equatorial to southern Africa. That means they are geographically dispersed descendants of shared ancestors. I don't find that too surprising. All considered.

Was it surprising when once, off the coast of Japan, a member of this species complex breached vertically up out of the water seventy times in a row (usually they do this only twice or three times)? Maybe everyone missed the message. Japan is the only area where one can still commercially hunt this whale.

Was it surprising when a member of the clade swallowed a white South African tour operator? (Not long enough to kill him, just long enough to change his outlook.) After the whale spit him back out, he said, "Everything went dark. I felt enormous pressure." The tourist industry says this swallowing incident was obviously definitely a mistake on the part of the whale. I'm not saying you can't trust those reports. I'm just saying that they come from the tourist industry, something we also know something about in the Caribbean.

Tropical whales engage in direct and complex actions that you can't explain away.

Like other baleen whales, this whale lives by gulping and filtering, mouth wide open to the ocean around them. Sometimes they breathe a rainbow. The size of their breath is the length of their whole bodies. Up to thirteen feet high. Sometimes they collaborate with seabirds, penguins, other whales, dolphins, and even sharks to catch fish in motion. But I am only an apprentice marine mammal. Still learning the complexity of my open mouth, the gulf of my lunging gulping longing to be related, the long mystery in the color of my breath. So what I wonder is what will we do with the complexity of our relation? Who will we teach a lesson, how will we make a statement, when will we collaborate? Could it be now? How do we honor our shared ancestors and our different situations? I'm asking because I honestly don't know. I'm early in this.

But if I could breathe a rainbow, I would grow myself towards you. I would brighten what's between us, filter nourishing possibilities. I would swallow worlds of yes. I would. I would open wide in trust and transformation. It is complex, how could it not be, how I am related to you, how you are relating to me, how we are relative across. But here it is, my open mouth, my whole body breath in color. Here it is, my lunge towards you, the discernment of my lungs. There you are, you wild rainbow. Here we go.

nine

learn from conflict

SOME SEA LIONS ONLY FIGHT for fifteen seconds but some suffering from disease outbreaks have begun to eat their own young. Looking at the responses of sea lions to species scale difficulties, I use this section to prompt us to learn from and be intentional about how the harms closest to home are both forcing and teaching us to evolve. How would we spend our time if we realized that the conflicts we are experiencing now urgently demand that we create a more loving world as soon as possible?

The rāpoka (sea lions) in Aotearoa have struggled since the 90s. Conservationists estimate that half of the population died since then. A disease broke out that killed 60 percent of pups and 20 percent of adults classified as female, and adults classified as male were observed killing and eating their young in striking numbers. Their own species is now on the list of species that threatens their species. So we have something in common.

Sea lions stake their claims on strips of beach and fight each other over them. They vocalize to keep each other from getting too close. The guidebooks say their threats are "ritualized postures," a particular form repeated. The guidebooks also have a name for this territorial behavior. They call it "tenure." Have you heard of that?

The Maori have a *taonga* or treasured relationship with the rāpoka recognized in the Ngāi Tahu claims Settlement Act of 1998 (the same year of the disease outbreak in fact), but which of course is part of a much older practice of ancestral listening and acknowledgement of spiritual communion beyond the human. I am grateful that Maōri leaders have fought for generations to participate in the strategies for relationship to the rāpoka population administered by colonial conservationists. Because in my heart I am still listening.

I love you. I know that those close to you have harmed you and that you have done the same, because I am close to you. I am still listening. And when you turn your words into a sharpened fence on shifting sand, I understand, and I hear more than you can say yet. And every time you risk a closeness that goes against all you were taught, I am here clapping. I am so grateful. You are here healing all of us.

South American sea lions fight each other sometimes, but not for more than fifteen seconds. I mean who has the time?

Living at the shoreline where vampire bats attack, where orcas sometimes beach themselves up out of the water just to eat their children, who really has more than fifteen seconds of bark or bite for their own community members? Someone somewhere has a worldstar stopwatch, watching, timing, how long will we fight each other?

Me, I would rather focus upward. Wouldn't you? I'm developing the muscle set to hold my head up high here at the edge. I know there's something up there besides the bats that wreck my sleep. Sea lions can regulate their own body temperatures. They know when they are too hot and what to do. They shift, recalibrate, and let it go in fifteen seconds or less. Could we get there?

Look. There is something above all of this that brought us here together. Can you see it? Can you hear it? And the sky is big enough for everything about you and me that makes no sense right now. Here, at the shoreline, the sky kisses the land and the horizon at the same time. Sometimes I strain to see the invisible, this air that holds me either way. But what a perfect place to study the unbound: here at the shoreline where you test my limits daily. And loving you can be the stretch that shapes the length of me, the strength of us. And yes, sometimes I have to vocalize my limits and so do you. Let's get it done though, and get back to breathing sky.

ten

honor your boundaries

A HOODED SEAL GETS EVERYTHING they need to travel the world from only four days of nursing. No one knows how the Baikal seal ended up in a freshwater lake. And Amazon dolphins in captivity may be dying from sleep deprivation. What are the boundaries that we choose and do not choose? What are the distances we need and what are the walls that that will isolate and destroy us? How can we discern the differences between generative boundaries and destructive borders? Are we ready to move towards nourishing forms of adaptation?

In four days the hooded seal gets everything she needs from the super-fat-rich milk of her mother. She survives any distance. She has what she needs. One young hooded seal traveled through the Atlantic over the Arctic seas and back down into the Pacific before scientists met her in California. Evidently this is common, which is why we are all over the world. Scientists call them vagrant juveniles, but we know better. A seal will exhale, submerge herself in the ocean and breathe through her whole body. Like this.

Amazon river dolphins have not done well in captivity. Less than 20 percent have been able to survive in aquariums worldwide. The record in the United States is even worse. According to the Audubon Society, out of seventy Amazon river, aka boto dolphins captured and housed in US aquariums between 1956 and 1966, only one survived into the mid-1980s.

What's the problem? First of all, freedom is a basic need and a divine imperative. As former poet laureate Tracy K. Smith said on her daily poetry podcast *The Slowdown*, "All animals allowed to live free and wild protect something holy in the world."[31] I agree. All animals. Including us.

And so what can those of us navigating layers of captivity, forced migration, and systemic involuntary adaptation learn from the specific experiences of the captive boto in the second half of the twentieth century?

Some zoo and conservation theorists say that the boto dolphins died of massive sleep deprivation. Dolphins generally "sleep with one eye open," as the saying goes, alternating halves of their brain to rest without drowning. Maybe you can relate?

31 Tracy K. Smith, *The Slowdown Podcast,* August 5, 2019.

And although scientists have not extensively observed or studied the sleep of Amazon river dolphins, some believe that the slope in the river bank is a resting place that supportively holds Amazon river dolphins while they are sleeping, unlike ocean dolphins who sleep in the middle of the water, without the support of the edges of land. Another way to say it is that the sleep deprivation that boto dolphins suffer in captivity is a result of a lack of the boundaries that helped them rest well at home. Is a lack of supportive boundaries impacting your sleep?

As a daughter of immigrant insomniacs who sleeps with one ear open, I think this question of sleep is crucial. As Black women artists, from Almah LaVon Rice-Faina to Shelly Davis Roberts to Patrisse Khan-Cullors to The Nap Ministry, are making abundantly clear, rest is resistance and sleep is political. Systemic nightmares threaten our sleep.

And the systems of harm that deprive us of restful boundaries are the exact same systems that enforce punitive borders where countless families are separated right now, caged, stressed and sleepless. The CIA has openly used sleep deprivation as an "interrogation practice" since 9/11. I agree with the psychologists and human rights activists who insist that sleep deprivation is a form of torture.

So, for decades, Amazon river dolphins have been subjected to captivity and torture. Mostly, they have not survived. What are the conditions of your sleep deprivation? What are the contours of your captivity? Does it offer something to your own torment to know you are not alone in your tiredness?

Could we, the restless, the overworked, the underslept, the one-eye-open wary sleepers, activate kinship through the dolphin adaptations we have already learned in order not to drown here? Could we imagine a world where we are all safe enough to sleep held in the arms of the river, in her mothering flow, supported by the boundaries we need to fully rest?

I want that for you. I want that for me. All this time that I have been half-awake, I have been dreaming of a world that could deserve you. They told me it was a hallucination, this waking dream I want for all of us, but now I know the truth. In a world where capitalism as usual makes us complicit in drowning the planet, we are the ones who are already dolphins, the psychics, the visionaries. We could trust ourselves. Our adaptable foreheads were not made to be caged; we deserve the restful freedom to evolve, to—as D'atra Jackson said at the North Carolina Emergent Strategy Immersion—"surrender to your dreams."

Yes. On the banks of this river, I surrender to the boundaries that land is teaching. Yes. I surrender to the demands of my dream for you and for myself. Which is love. Which is abundant rest. Which is a visionary world that looks so much like a dream, but when you close one eye, it opens. When you open up this close to the edge, land holds you and water moves through you. And what you thought was closed off to you opens up like possibility. And the danger you thought would open up and swallow you and everyone you love instead reclarifies who you are, updates your dreams and waits to wake you with new purpose.

If I can learn to sleep it is because my dreams are yours and for you and of us. It is because my love is an ocean, but my path is a river shaped by land that will heal us if we let it. And it flows back into the ocean anyway. Before all of this, there was a deep Black dream that woke as us. And we are the ones in-between enough, dream-eyed enough, exhausted enough to remember.

There are a few theories as to how the Baikal seal ended up in Siberia in a lake far away from all their other saltwater seal relatives. Some say half a million years ago they were separated from the other seals by expanding and contracting ice sheets. Some say there is an underground channel into Baikal Lake (the deepest lake in the world) that no one has seen.

What is for sure is that the Baikal seal has adapted to fresh water with glistening Black grace. Round and shining. They have two extra liters of blood, which allow them to breathe underwater longer. Long enough to mate underwater, scientists guess, because no one has seen them. They are the only mammal in the lake ecology and are now indispensable to their interspecies community.

Sometimes I wonder how I got here too. How did I change to learn to breathe here? What did I lose? What would I be like if there never was a break between me and those on the other side of the passage? And is it enough, this one deep lake, for all the life I have to live?

The Baikal seal (Russian name "*nerpa*") reminds me that, right where I am, I am connected to all. And the Blackness of me glimmering like stars communicates in all directions. And the roundness of me, sleek as blubber, is Earth herself fully embraced by a Black universe.

And please remember that I love you no matter what happened between us, no matter what took me from you or you from me. Across the continents of ice, this lake has deep and loving boundaries. And I am so fully held and nourished. You can trust that I am where I need to be.

What does it mean for scientists to say a whale is "shy"? Giant beaked whales (of which there may be three different species) are a major whale mystery. The conservation status is "data deficient." Seems like for scientists, there is knowing and then there is knowing.

In the case of a "new" species of giant beaked whale that Philip Morin, of the National Oceanic and Atmospheric

Association (NOAA [they pronounce it *Noah* isn't that biblical apocalyptic and cute?]), is investigating, there are contra-
dictions. According to Morin, the whale is so mysterious that
it has never been seen alive. He told the BBC that it is rare
for it to even wash up on shore if it dies. "If they do die..."
he said, "they are far away from shore." (Does that mean he
thinks that it's possible that they don't die?) I'm here for the
mystery as much as anyone else. But I wonder sometimes
about the manufacture of novelty. Especially since, in the
same article, the local Japanese people who live near where
three of these "mystery" whales stranded, say of course they
have seen that whale species before and it's called *karasu*, or
raven, because it is Black.

There is a difference between being shy and being selective.
I would say that another whale described under the name giant beaked whale, the southern four-toothed whale (which
the conservationists and guidebooks call "shy"), may just
practice stealth. It's not the same thing. "Teeth may flash in
sunlight," the *Smithsonian Guide* says about this whale. And
though I love the mystique, it makes me wonder. Sometimes
when someone is avoiding you, they are just avoiding you.
We have the right to be obscure. It is not an invitation to
colonize us. It is not seduction. Boundaries can be so beautiful. Teach so much. This is a whale that is Black but sometimes wears enough algae to appear brown or orange at sea
on the move. Once a group of these whales who were being
followed by scientists stayed underwater for an hour, traveled
four miles without surfacing. Do you think the researchers
got the hint?

What I know is that I love you. Even if you are not interested in being followed. Even if you show up in disguises.
Even if I'm not the one who should know you or name you
or classify you at all. And I celebrate your right to evade and
avoid me. I celebrate your journey however deep, however
long. I respect you as so much bigger than my own understanding. And me too. I don't have to be available to be el-
igible for breath. I don't have to be measurable in a market

of memes. I don't have to be visible to be viable on my path. I don't have to be shy to be sacred about my time. There are only two things I have to do, my mom taught me, and I can do them in the company of my choosing. The company of myself, my living, my dead, my folks, my dreams. 1. Stay Black; 2. Breathe.

eleven

respect your hair

ONE OF THE MAJOR THINGS I found when I studied guidebooks about marine mammals was that much of the same
language that fuels racism, gendered binaries, and other
forms of oppression shows up in "scientific" descriptions of
marine mammals. Most of these descriptions are also written by white western men. This section looks at the hair of
seals, walruses, and whales in connection with hair discourses
within our species in order to reclaim the bodily feature most
entangled with racial definition (after skin).

Inspired by Bob Marley's quote, "Trust the universe and
respect your hair," I am interested in a marine-mammal attuned redefinition of hair as a life-giving technology. What
does hair mean? What does it protect? And how we could
honor hair as both a boundary and teacher?

The scientific name for the ringed seal (*Pusa hispida*) is a description of her hair, which is more "bristly" than that of other seals. "Bristly" if we're being nice. The Latin meanings for "*hispida*" range from bristly to dirty, to rough, shaggy, etc.

In diaspora they say it twice. The most geographically dispersed subspecies is called *Pusa hispida hispida*. So her hair is, in the words of the National Audubon Society, "stiffer" than that of other seals.

I say good for her. I applaud the adaptation. Remember she lives in ice. Remember she is the favorite food of polar bears. Hunted by walruses and orcas and people. She could at least make herself sharp. Eventually.

Her first coat is white and woolly. The one she is born in. And almost no one sees it, because her mother is hiding her in ice. And then, in a few weeks, she sheds to become Black and silver. Capable of depth and diving. Glistening and dark like the cold sea. It is only after her first annual molt that she gets her beautiful rings, and starts to pose, as if Mickalene Thomas was going to paint her. Iridescence of skin. Collage and mirage. The Iñupiat call her *natchek*. The Yupik-speaking Inuit people of the Bering Strait call her *niknik*. Or sometimes my favorite, *netsiavinerk*, meaning silver jar. Because it's magical to be so textured and Black, so sleek and silver, so sharp to the touch.

And if you too have been called out of your name. If that wise evolving art you have used to distinguish and protect yourself, not to be touched by predators, your hair, your language, your leaving. If they have used your hair to find and then dismiss you, your curl, your cut, your weaving. If they have lied about their secret wishes to emulate your diamond in the ocean way of living. Do not despair.

I am with you. And I love your wise audacious boundaries. I love your visible evolution. I love your decadent adaptation in a world of watered mouths. I love your bristle and your backbone. The way you breathe through your whole body. The way you can freeze onlookers with your eyes and build worlds out of edge and frost and melt. You work of art.

You magic bell. You jar of genius. Map of galaxies. You goad the world to roughen texture. Tempt the sky to fall in rings.

One of the top ten truths I love about walruses? Their deciphering faces. Their whiskers, or vibrissae, are a highly evolved adaptation that they can use to distinguish between tiny items in the sea floor sediment. This thick facial hair allows them to locate buried clams quickly during their average six-minute dives underwater. Mother walruses know their babies best by touching them with their whiskers. They don't depend on their eyes. They trust intimate vibration.

What a way of knowing. How you breathe, how you move, through my breath, I let my face teach me you. In the deep swirl of dirt, I trust the smallest vibration to feed me and us. Evolved hair as a sensitive technology. The hair on my face as unplucked oracle. Shaped transmission.

Could we study that? What if I was so adept at the meaning of the movement of my hairs that I could know the small difference between yes and no? Between here and not here? Between stay and leave now? What if I know you by the movements I can sense in you through goosebumps, the way my hair stands up and greets you, or calms down? There is a vibration all around my skin and my hair is touching it, telling me something I usually ignore. But what if I remembered that my living depends on knowing what is what here in the dirt that I can't see through? Here in the depth where I must find what is hidden? Here on your skin where every message waits for me?

I love the wild technology of your face. What it says and tells and keeps. I honor the sensitivity of your small significant decisions. I trust the growing genius of your hair, how it protects you, how it reaches, how it moves and measures movement. I would study the invisible. Sometimes I can't trust what I see. But listen. Small, more slight than breath. Yes. That. That. Do you feel it?

The fact that you grew up not knowing that narwhals were a real animal swimming around in the Arctic right now, is not a coincidence. It is the result of a long and lucrative conspiracy. Turns out, since the Middle Ages, whalers, traders, explorers, and even chemists collaborated to hide the existence of the narwhal as a real animal, while selling their tusks as "unicorn horns" at a huge profit. It makes me think about the ways enforced marginality and increased profit margins have been linked to each other for a long time.

It makes me think about who benefited all this time from the conspiracy to pretend I didn't exist. And then later the lie that the only real part of me was the part they could sell.

I certainly know who was harmed. I was. Those who would behead me knowingly sacrificed me to a lucrative idea, while also banishing the threat of my actual magic. Who was harmed? You were. You suffered the tragedy of trading the actual accountable magic of the planet for a myth about specialness, you choked your own self with enough heter-onormative fairytales to fund generations of delusions. We were harmed. All of us. Because there is blood in the water at the limit of our dreams. The ways we are cut off have conse-quences. And the market circles.

One day, after studying whale sounds at the Aquarium of the Pacific, my partner and I bought a puzzle for our nieces of Emily Winfield Martin's *Dream Narwhal* painting.

We wanted it because of the impossible and very real whale that is depicted and because of the impossible and very real Black girl in the image, breathing underwater, looking forward in her dreams. My oldest niece, an animal guide-book in herself, was two years old at the time and as she put the puzzle together she said "bonita, bonita," and lovingly touched the painted hair.

Who benefited from the conspiracy to teach us that we were not beautiful? That we were not possible? Who first turned our adaptation into profit? Our deep sharp realness into fairytale dust to sell back to us when we noticed ourselves, turning that prior scarcity of representation into a very high profit margin for whom? Ask the narwhal. Supply and demand work over time that way. Make you happy to buy what you already have.

At just the right moment, the scholar Tavia Nyong'o reminded me that to conspire means to breathe together. Like narwhals do by the hundreds every summer. It's happening now. May we activate and renew the oldest conspiracy, remember all the thick impossible breathing before us and after us and with us, too real to be for sale. Too beautiful to be forgotten. Too magical for theft.

I am still unlearning the coping mechanisms I created when I thought I was impossible within myself. And the equally harmful tactics I internalized when I believed the tokenizing myth that I was, and should be the only one of my kind. And now all I want is to breathe together. For we are real with a power beyond commodified magic (even commodified Black Girl Magic and representational gifts).

We are real. We are beyond. When we conspire with our ancestors to honor our dreams. When we tap into the part of us that is not for sale, so unmarketable that the capitalists say it don't exist, but it do. It is you. It is all of us. I love you. My realest dream. My wildest truth. You beautiful puzzle. The air I breathe.

twelve

end capitalism

I GUESS I COULD HAVE started here. Let me be clear: the actual suffering and endangerment of marine mammals on the planet right now is caused by the extractive, destructive processes and consequences of capitalism. The meditations in this section look at the vaquita and the Atlantic right whale, which are on the brink of extinction because the commercial fishing industry finds it expensive and inconvenient to change their practices. We look at the fate of the striped dolphin and Greece's attempt to save its economy by allowing dangerous oil drilling in their habitat. We ponder the strange state of the world where impoverished individual fishers actually kill marine mammals because they perceive them as threatening competition in a fishing market where they already can't compete. These are all examples of what capitalism means on an interspecies scale. At the same time, this section uplifts a former lobsterman who risked and gave his life as part of a crew of people who untangle right whales from deadly nets, and an Indigenous-owned fishing company that is actively fighting against the extinction of the New Zealand white front dolphin, as hope and instruction towards moving into right relationship with the planet and each other by ending capitalism as soon as possible.

I wonder if we could outgrow rope. Braided with blood, a tangled legacy. Could we at this point, evolve past nets of capture, the intersecting technology of getting and keeping. I'm asking for a friend. Vaquita, who EcoWatch says is days away from extinction all because of the pervasive use of gill-nets where she lives. And I'm asking for the North Atlantic right whale, also very close to extinction, whose major cause of death is getting caught in ropes used by large fishing vessels in her range. Or being stabbed by their propellers.

Neither of these species is having problems reproducing. North Atlantic right whales actually have a lot of reproductive sex and even more social sex just because.

The precarious status of the northern right whale is due to the fact that commercial whalers specifically targeted and hunted them for the entire period of the slave trade. But no one is hunting them now. In fact, recently, Joe Howlett, a lobster fisherman and member of a team of people who risk their lives trying to untangle these whales from the ropes that kill them, died in the process. Is it possible to untangle the consequences of centuries of rapacious greed?

The threat against the most critically endangered cetaceans on the planet (and most endangered marine mammals at this point) is a supposedly unintentional by-product of fishing as usual. Could the large fishing boats in the Atlantic become mindful enough to sense and avoid an animal as big and slow moving as the North Atlantic right whale (which actually was named the "right whale" specifically because it was slow moving and large enough to easily hunt from large ships with the technology they had two hundred years ago)? To hear the industry tell it, it's expensive and difficult. They say the necessary technology is years if not decades away. In other words, it may be available after the North Atlantic right whale is already extinct.

And what about the gillnets in the tiny range of the vaquita? They are already illegal, and the fishers who use them are impoverished people without other economic options at this time.

end capitalism /// 103

So Alexis, are you saying that to save these animals we have to not only abolish the commercial fishing industry, which is one of the major food sources on the planet, but also abolish capitalism itself THIS WEEK so no one needs to use an illegal gillnet or starve?

In a word? Yes.

But maybe you already know something about this. About how a deadly system doesn't have to seem like it's targeting you directly to kill you consistently. How, for example, long after the era of photographed lynchings where picnickers sliced off body parts and kept them as keepsakes, a system can still cut off parts of you daily, steal parts of yourself that you need, just in its daily functioning in the legacy of its original purpose. Maybe you think this is not about you (if so, that's a part that already went numb).

One female North Atlantic right whale was stabbed by a propeller as a baby and didn't die until fourteen years later when she was pregnant. As she expanded to hold life, her wound reopened, got infected, and killed her. Or think of Punctuation (this is what the researchers who have been studying this whale for forty years call her), a grandmother North Atlantic right whale who died in the summer of 2019. She had given birth eight times, survived entanglement five different times, and had scars from multiple boat strikes and propellers. And at least three of her children died from entanglement before she died. Maybe you know something about what it means to bear the constant wounding of a system that says it's about something else entirely. It might sound hollow to you too when you hear these deaths are not the point, that these deaths are just a by-product that cannot be prevented for the sake of the system. Surely there must be some way to improve the system that already exists.

I don't think so. Where are the people who argue that commercial fishing is necessary for human life when the same economic system pollutes that exact food supply and raises carbon to levels that are killing fish off already? None of these things can be separated from each other. We are all entangled.

And the fact that entanglement is a slow death doesn't make it any better; it in fact makes it more gruesome. And I mourn the parts of you that lost feeling today. I mourn the scars you will not notice until you have a reason to grow. I mourn the freedom you don't know because these ropes have been here longer than you have been and big or small you can't evade them.

If we don't do it, if we don't end capitalism this week, it is because we are entangled, a reality that will continue to wound us after the vaquita and the North Atlantic right whale disappear off the face of the Earth. So you don't have to save the whales, but at least take a look at the ropes. Acknowledge what has already been severed, the costs of this system as usual. At least take a moment to imagine how you would move if we weren't all caught up in this. Could we do that? I'm asking for myself. And if you can at all feel these last two sentences, then maybe it's not impossible: I love you. You deserve to be free.

The striped dolphin (*Stenella coeruleoalba*) got sum to say.[32] She's sick and tired. Of being sick and tired.[33] She's been dealing with cycles of viruses that kill her species by the thousands and that are recurring in the Atlantic, Pacific, and Mediterranean. A social, deep-water dolphin, the striped dolphin is vulnerable to cetacean disease outbreaks. If pilot whales have it, striped dolphins will get it. Researchers don't know the exact cause of the virus yet, but it killed one thousand dolphins in the Mediterranean Sea from 1990 to 1992, and came back in 2007 and again in 2019. One factor

---

32 This is an Outkast reference.
33 Quoth the divine Fannie Lou Hamer.

that I'm sure doesn't help is the pollution of the striped dolphin's habitat.

For example, right now in Greece, oil companies are scrambling to drill in marine-mammal protected areas, namely the deepest area of the Mediterranean Sea, where the striped dolphins live. A conservative (but not conservationist) Greek government that sees ocean drilling as the solution to all of Greece's economic problems is welcoming even the most reckless oil drillers to their shores. Of course, these politicians are not talking about the major potential costs of even a small oil spill in their region, not only for the marine mammals who live there, but also for the government itself and Greece's own tourist industry. I am writing this in solidarity with the Greek activists who are currently using music and community education to raise awareness and stop off-shore drilling speculation.

Because I know what it feels like to be sick of systemic oppression and its cycles of extraction. The virus impacting these dolphins presses on their lungs, their brains. They struggle to breathe, they swim in strange circles. They end up far off course in a place that can't sustain them. Do you know something about this?

I too have been moving in circles, confused. I too have been struggling to breathe. I too have wondered how did I get so far from what my body and spirit need. And I thought I was done writing about striped dolphins, but so many of us are dizzy and labored, bewildered and estranged. So what would I say if I was a striped dolphin?

I love you. And even on your sickest, saddest day you deserve an ocean as blue as your name. You deserve a safety as deep as your need. You deserve food, community, school, and home. And you were not wrong to associate with your kindred. And you were not wrong to breathe loud about what you believed. And the dizziness you feel is justified. We are living in a world off course. And the pressure in your lungs is urgency. We have to learn the language of this air. We are sick of these tired cycles of economic vulnerability, resource grabs, and waste and harm spiraling down. We are ready to breathe differently. And evolve.

Round. Tūpoupou, also known as the New Zealand white front dolphin, also known as *Cephalorhynchus hectori* is round. Not only due to the way she curves around herself and dives, but also because her distinctive fins and flippers are round. Her face is round with no differentiated beak. She is the smallest, rarest dolphin on the planet. Does that stop her from being connected to everything? No.

Turns out the world is round.

Right now there are only about 1,500 of these dolphins left surrounding the islands of Aotearoa, which is the only place in the world where she lives. Does that stop her from being connected to everything? No. The world is round.

Right now, the largest Maori-owned fishing company is partnering with wildlife conservationists on internal and external transformations to honor the lives and living space of the tūpoupou and Māui dolphins who live on their shorelines. This fishing company, named Moana, paid the World Wildlife Federation (WWF) to consult on a holistic change to their fishing nets, boats, and practices designed to stop drowning marine mammals. Moana is also one of two major fishing companies in Aotearoa partnering with WWF to change the national policy to protect dolphins more rigorously and effectively.

It's rare to see a commercial entity do its inner work and take public action in honor of a species outside of its consumer base. In fact, in most instances, dolphins, the great fishers that they are, are de facto competitors of fishing companies. But who wants an ocean without them? Remember, the world is round.

Although part of my marine mammal apprenticeship offering is my complete divestment from the fishing industry, I have respect for Moana and other fishing companies that understand that, while in the short run species seem to compete, in the long run, every species is necessary. An ecological approach is ethical. The range of costs to consider are not on the scale of a single species. I'm sure neither Moana nor the WWF are perfect, and no, I don't believe that capitalism can heal the Earth, but there is something for me to learn from this rare collaboration across these particular sectors.

And it reminds me that if a fishing company can do its inner and outer work on a national scale, I can most certainly remember the connection between my inner transformations and my actions in the world. I can, you can become more than a market. I can, you can remember that the world is round. What we touch, how we steer, the roundness is the measure of our purposeful living. The impact is always beyond one species. We are not competing for space on this Earth. We are, at our best, learning to connect towards the possibility of remaining. We are at our best, generous because we know the planet has already been more generous with us than we could ever earn.

Round. The world is round like an embrace, and you touch everything. And I love the ways you are learning reach and reflection. I love the ways you are forgetting our education into enemy status at home. The world is round. Everything comes around and remembers you. I remember you. With love.

thirteen

refuse

AND THEN THERE ARE THE marine mammals that have most effectively escaped observation. For example:

> • the deep diving beaked whales, many of which have never been positively identified by western scientists,
> • the Atlantic gray whales who disappeared during the slave trade and have just recently reappeared,
> • and the Hawaiian monk seals who are regenerating themselves on military bases that have shut down in the archipelago.

In conversation with theorists Saidiya Hartman, Hortense Spillers, Wahneema Lubiano, Kevin Quashie, and Eric Stanley, this section honors what it means to refuse to be seen, to be known, to participate when politics as we know them have prioritized recognition by and access to the dominant paradigm. What becomes possible when we are immersed in the queerness of forms of life that dominant systems cannot chart, reward, or even understand?

Like too many great artists and most beaked whales, the Antillean/Gulf Stream beaked whale is only recognized after its death. Scientists have never "positively identified" one at sea, but it's the most likely toothed whale to strand on western North Atlantic shores. So all scientific study of this species of whale is based on dissections of found dead bodies. Despite this complete absence of living witness, the *Smithsonian* says something about sex distinction at sea. It seems they cannot help themselves: "The female is probably impossible to identify at sea [it seems Hortense Spillers and Saidiya Hartman taught me something about this too...][34] and males are likely to be exceedingly difficult." And I wonder.

But mostly I just applaud in complete admiration. A fugitive you cannot find a record for is the most successful fugitive of all. What a victory, that at least you, my kin, have completely protected your living existence from western science for this whole time. What an elegant and thorough example of living well.

And all my love to you who preserve the mysteries. Whom the empire of binaries will never define. All of you who love with a depth beyond recognition, nurturing freedom over understandability, valuing life as so much more important than simple comprehension. Thank you. Thank you for loving me without even knowing what on Earth I am.

34 See Hortense Spillers, "Mama's Baby, Papa's Maybe: An American Grammar Book" in *Black, White and In Color: Essays on American Literature and Culture* (Chicago: University of Chicago Press, 2003), 203–29; and Saidiya Hartman, "Venus in Two Acts" in *Small Axe: A Caribbean Journal of Criticism* 12, no. 2 (2008): 1–14.

There is a quiet whale who doesn't jump or show tail. Who breathes softly and speaks low. *Balaenoptera acutorostrata* (the winged whale with the sharp face, called minke for bad reasons) is so low-key scientists once called them the "silent whale." They don't show themselves much at the surface, they change direction underwater and frustrate trackers. But bio-acoustic researchers have been listening. In the Pacific and in the West Indies, microphones await any sound.

There are few. In the Pacific, a study recently recorded a grunt and a small sound they described as running fingers over a comb. The first sounds ever recorded from the subspecies in that area. In the Caribbean, the sounds are at such a low frequency that they have to be sped up by a factor of ten to be audible. Researchers are interested because the "boing" sound some species make is unique among whales as far as they know. As of this writing, scientists also worry that man-made ocean noise pollution will drown their voices out completely.[35]

The quiet of the hunted is learned. Bioacoustic researchers aren't the only ones listening. So are orcas who regularly hunt this smallest of rorqual whales. So they speak quietly and carefully organize themselves in groups. They have one of the most complex levels of social organization (by sex, age, reproductive condition) of any whale. When alone, they organize anyway, sharing space and respecting hunting boundaries. They've kept observation of their mating—even their child–parent relationships—from researchers. But again, all of this organization happens quietly. What would Kevin Quashie say?[36] The quiet of the hunted. Is it sovereign?

The name scientists use for this whale is "minke," supposedly in reference to an inexperienced whaler named Meincke, who suggested that hunting these whales would be a good idea. For commercial purposes, other whalers considered

35 Https://www.sciencemag.org/news/2020/02/minke-whales-are
-struggling-communicate-over-din-ocean-noise.

36 See Kevin Quashie, *The Sovereignty of Quiet: Beyond Resistance in Black Culture* (New Brunswick, NJ: Rutgers University Press, 2012).

them too small to bother with, but once they'd decimated the populations of larger whales, these too-small relatives became the main target of the whaling industry. Right now they are the only commercially hunted baleen whale. Maybe it is better to be quiet than to call me the name of the first would-be-assassin. Whoever wished me dead in the name of capital is not equipped to name me. Your name is not my name. What am I saying?

There are low-frequency sounds that have been recorded for years and just recently attributed to the hunted one with wings, sharp of mouth, sleek of movement. What are they saying right now that reaches us as a rumble we don't know we're hearing, an organizing vibration of action unclaimed? What am I saying below the register of those who could use anything I say against me? What do I say? Maybe my name. Maybe I'm saying my true name. Maybe I'm quietly living my name. Hush and you can learn it. Be moved by what you can't name. Transformed by quiet intention. And know that you do not know. Who said that? Move.

Here in the spotted Atlantic, surveillance is everywhere. It's the water we breathe. The drowning context of being so gorgeous, so wanted. Or as my friend Eric Stanley says of the problem of recognition and Anti-Trans Optics: "how can we be seen without being known and how can we be known without being hunted?"[37]

Ask the Atlantic spotted dolphin, which is not always spotted actually. Only the eldest of the species have spots, and the dynamic of having spots sometimes, of being differently

---

37 See Eric A. Stanley, "Anti-Trans Optics: Recognition, Opacity, and the Image of Force" in *South Atlantic Quarterly* 116, no. 3 (2017): 612–20.

marked over a lifetime, has made these dolphins hard to identify. The *Smithsonian* says they have "puzzled experts for a
long time." And because of this, and maybe also because of
their epic hang time when they jump out of the ocean, they
are very much sought after. For example, in 1995, an Atlantic
spotted dolphin got stranded on the shore in Texas. Texan
scientists, of course, detained them (this is a singular them),
but eventually let them loose, with a wire in their dorsal fin to
spy on other dolphins in the gulf and out beyond it. The scientists called it help. And in a way, it was. And I know some
of us can relate, because to access any service (including the
social media that I used to share these words originally) we
submit to being tracked and monitored. This spotted ecology
ain't no easy place to swim.

One other thing though: the Atlantic spotted dolphin,
so acrobatic, agile, quick, whetted the dreams of Sea-World-
esque captors early on. And though I hear a whole group
of these dolphins have been consensually communing with
people in the Bahamas since the 1970s, leaving and coming back when they want, the guidebooks say that "they
generally do not acclimate well to captive conditions and
are therefore not popular in the display industry." Hmm.
Sounds like what Wahneema Lubiano taught us about: a
cover story that covers something up.[38] Because the lack of
acclimation, the early deaths, the frequent still-births, the
listless living of dolphins and whales in captivity has generally not stopped the industry from capturing them anyway.
So what is it about the Atlantic spotted dolphin that is effectively evasive? How can I become unpopular to those who
would enslave me?

I see you too, you wireless hunter with your hooks in all
my movements. And I know somewhere in your lust lives a

38 See Wahneema Lubiano, "Black Ladies, Welfare Queens, and State
Minstrels: Ideological War by Narrative Means," in *Race-ing Justice,
Engendering Power*, edited by Toni Morrison (New York: Pantheon
Books, 1992).

desire to get this deep. May all your love outlive your lies, beloved predator.

And for the sweet stealth acrobats who exhaust systems with our constant transformation, who are mistaken every day for something else. Yes. All my love. And keep on going.

The *Smithsonian* says that the Hawaiian monk seal and the Caribbean monk seal are "separated sisters" with a continent between them. In fact, in the first naming of a new seal genus in over a century, researchers in 2014 created the genus *Neomonachus* to describe the closeness in evolutionary relationship between these two species of monk seals (one extinct and one that is classified as one of the most endangered marine mammals on the planet) and to distinguish them from the Mediterranean monk seal, who the *Smithsonian* now describes as not a sister, but "a distant cousin."

Scientists estimate that the two "New world" seal species split off from their "Old world" cousin (this is still the *Smithsonian*'s language) about six million years ago. The split between the Caribbean and Hawaiian seals is more recent. About three million years. Colonialism has had a devastating impact on both the Hawaiian and the Caribbean species. I wonder about the ongoing life of their ancestral connection. And sisterhood and solidarity and the important decolonial direct actions taking place in the Caribbean (especially in Puerto Rico) and in Hawaii (especially in protection of sacred Mauna Kea).

I write elsewhere in this book about the Caribbean monk seal, which scientists have declared extinct. Conservationists feel that the close relationship between the Hawaiian and Caribbean monk seals is even more of a reason to do everything possible to prevent the extinction of the Hawaiian monk seal, the closest living relative of an extinct species.

One of the worst impacts of the population crisis among these seals is what the guidebook calls the "mobbing" of female seals by male seals. We would call it rape, deadly rape, which threatens the population even more. Conservationists have actually captured, removed, and relocated male seals for this reason. There is also now a seal hospital in Hawaii with rehabilitative services specifically for seals.

In heartening news, the Hawaiian monk seal population has increased 3 percent every year for the last five. Looks like one of the best things to happen for the Hawaiian monk seal population was the closing of two US military bases at Sand Island and Kure Atoll. Monk seals have reclaimed the sites and their populations there have steadily increased. According to the guidebooks, the Hawaiian monk seal populations on those islands had disappeared because they "appear to be intolerant of human presence." Intolerant of military presence at least.

I think often about the consequences of colonialism within a threatened group. The cost of losing almost everything. The impact of military normalcy. The multiple violences we endure. What if the path to conservation of any of species remaining on the planet is demilitarization? What is the solidarity, evolutionary sistering, ancestral imperative called for in this moment where US colonial territories are in active refusal? What does it look like to be intolerant of colonialism? What life would spring up, what recovery is possible if the colonial force actually shuts down? I'm asking for a sister of mine, wherever she is now. Three million years ago she taught me something about us. I haven't forgotten. We deserve to be free.

Boto, the "pink dolphin" who lives in the Amazon River Basin, is actually pink and blue. She lives at the confluence of rivers and mythologies and so she is flexible. She can change the shape of her head and look in all directions. You can sometimes hear her breathing loud, projecting air up taller than six feet, but usually they say her breathing sounds more like a sigh.

No babies are pink. No. Pink comes with time. And anyway what we call pink is the blood all through, the capillaries so close to the surface they sing. The Janelle Monae of it all. All visibly vulnerable, meaning brave. Meaning move my blood where it is needed in the turbid water of change. Pink, as in ready. And hunted.

Since I live here, at the confluence, I cannot afford to hide. Instead my very breathing is critique. It takes up space. It moves my blood. To where I need. You see my living and you think it is my skin. And underneath, I am a muscle of response and shifting shape. I am. I am. And I am who I need to be. I am not hiding.

Know that I love you in a world that would turn your blood into candy. Criminalize your flexibility. Oversimplify your claim to your own life. Know that for me your blood is a scripture. I want it to stay in your veins. I am saying your name. We're not breathing in vain.

Chanel Scurlock. Johana Medina Leon. Chynal Lindsey. Layleen Polanco. Zoe Spears. Presente.[39]

Out in the ocean it is not considered queer for bottlenose

---

39 These are the names of trans women of color murdered in the weeks and months leading up to Pride Month 2019.

#shesafewesafe #Blacktranswomenmatter

dolphins assigned male by scientists to live in bonded pairs for decades, whole lifetimes. It is common. It is not considered queer for groups of bottlenose dolphins that scientists call "related females" to travel the whole world together for always. It is common. And these are the lives of the most "common" dolphins. The archetypal dolphins. Flipper and them. As a species that is hardly consistent about anything (they eat whatever, they live wherever, they give birth anytime, their skin could be dark or light, they show up in all different sizes), they consistently remember each other. They have the longest social memory of anyone we've noticed; they know each other's whistles after decades apart. So we could call who they stay with an active commitment. Often a "same sex" commitment.

In captivity? Well that's something else.

All my love to the queers claiming ocean on land. To the brave ones here salting the rest of the Earth by building our uncommon lives around each other. We feel buoyant on illegal terms. We prioritize each other over the gravity of socially enforced narratives, laws and tax structures. We act on the knowledge that everything could change and yet if I was choosing I would choose you again.

We will all be marine mammals soon. So thank you for remembering to swim despite everything.

Gray whales are world shapers. The only large whale to feed on sediment on the bottom of the ocean, they leave massive trails on the underwater surface of the Earth. They dig up nutrients that feed whole ecosystems. And they have been missing from the Atlantic Ocean since the end of the transatlantic slave trade.

What happened? Marine biologists say it is still a mystery why the Atlantic population of gray whales went extinct. Is it possible that whalers on enslaving ships killed gray whales and didn't report it? Was there already a smaller population of gray whales than they had thought? Miscalculation and under-documentation are the theories so far. And no one mentions the timing of the transatlantic slave trade as relevant to the extinction of Atlantic gray whales. But me. And maybe others like me who can't help but think of slavery and our kin.

I wonder. Yes. I wonder if the toxicity of the slave trade and its impact on the ocean have been under-reported. Lucille Clifton says the "Atlantic is a sea of bones."[40] What is the half-life of the transubstantiation of life into servitude? Does it ever dissolve? And the bones of those captives who freed themselves, or left their bodies and were subsequently thrown overboard became...what? Sediment. Filtered ultimately into the baleen of the Atlantic gray whale, right? So there is actually a digestive truth to the idea that the ancestors we lost in the transatlantic slave trade became whales.

Is sediment sentient? Kriti Sharma is embarking on an underwater research project about micro-organisms in deep sea sediment that processes methane in a way that could re-balance the planet. Don't sleep on sediment, at the bottom, knowledge grows.

And maybe there is more to the interspecies relation. Could there have been an interspecies pact between those who would not survive the transatlantic slave trade? Could it be that a refusal to survive the slave trade could be transferred between species? Did the gray whales act out of solidarity, refusing the terms of a betrayal they held in their stomachs? Or, since researchers have recently discovered that gray whales can migrate between the Atlantic and Pacific oceans, did the Atlantic gray whales simply leave the Atlantic in response to their intimate knowledge of what exactly is at the bottom of slavery and join the Pacific population? An allergy to the marrowed loss? A repulsion for the latticed flesh?

---

40 See Lucille Clifton, "Atlantic is a Sea of Bones" in *Next: New Poems* (New York: BOA Editions, 1989).

And guess what? In 2013, 205 years after the abolition of the transatlantic slave trade (not slavery itself, but the transatlantic trade), a gray whale appeared in the Atlantic, off the coast of Namibia to the shock of whale watchers. And along the Atlantic today, and many days, my kin greet the ocean in ceremony including ritual blessings and cleansings of the descendants of those who did survive the transatlantic slave trade, those of us who also may be related to those parents, siblings, cousins, lovers who did not survive.

If the gray whale is ready to return to the Atlantic, am I? What is the clarity of my digestion, my knowledge of what can nourish life and what cannot? What in me will not tolerate the intolerable? What is the trajectory of my underwater trail? My mark on the planet, my refusal? The body of a gray whale is like a map. A plane of scars, barnacles, and lice. A living environment itself, replete with evidence. And could I ask myself with every decision, every complicity and move, what is at the bottom of this? What indentation am I making on the surface of this Earth, even if it is so far underwater no one can see?

At the bottom, there is love so complicated that it doesn't dissolve, and yet we can't digest it. At the bottom, there are choices even if they seem microscopic in scale. At the bottom, who you were and what you were became a whale and please come back to me with all your scars and patterns. I will seek you at the bottom of myself and breathe you up out of my crown. I will remember you and breathe your stolen breath. It is not small what happened to tear us apart. It is not over either. At the bottom: greed. But my love is textured, massive, scarred. My love is breathing, writing, path. My love is made from who you are. My love, I hear you in my gut. And so I stay and so I leave and you return.

There is a mystery species of *ziphiid* (beaked whale). One guidebook says "almost nothing known," another says "nothing is known for certain." Seems like they are the only *ziphiid* with teeth. Maybe they travel in small groups that are "extremely difficult to detect." Or maybe they are, like you, deep divers who spend "little time at the surface." One thing is for sure: there is no evidence of this whale ever getting caught up in anyone else's fishing gear or becoming available for any human use.

I call it wisdom. The inner capacity that allows a mammal to breathe undetected on a world such as this. Could I ever learn to be so unencumbered, forsaking my lust for the surface? And what would I find at the bottom of this while no one was saying my name?

All my love to the depth mammals. You who have learned to slow your breathing, take your time, be where you are, move undetected in a world so drunk on recognition that we drown. May we all inspire mystery, an approach to the divine, reminders with our very being that indeed "nothing is known for certain." That's right. "Almost nothing is known" at all. But know this one thing: I love you deep right where you are. And not because I know. This love is bigger than all that. I love you because you are as Black and unknowable as the universe myself. I love you most of all because I wonder.

fourteen

surrender

AND WHAT HAPPENS IF WE just let go? Like dolphins who
beach themselves on shore to eat, and trust the tide to bring
them back into the water, or who time their birth cycles to
seasonal floods, or migrate across the world following warm
currents on a menopausal planet. What it would take to
tune in with our environment enough to be in flow with the
Earth, instead of in struggle against it. Inspired by the evolution of the extinct prehistoric *Livyatan melvillei* (so-called sea
monster ancestor of the contemporary sperm whale), from
the being with the largest sharpest teeth to a being who uses
those same teeth not to kill or even to chew, but to listen, I
wonder if we, or the species that comes after us can turn our
weapons into weathervanes in time.

Most Black-and-white dolphins live at the shoreline. They collaborate to push sardines out onto the sand and then follow them to eat, stranding themselves on the beach for a while and then letting the waves take them back. Could I trust myself that much? And remember to breathe? Here on the shoreline, could I know in my gut that my home will reclaim me? That the dry spells will end? That the risks we take together are worthwhile impermanence? Because indeed we are vulnerable to Sea World opportunists. And sometimes we do get caught up.

I am learning to trust myself here at the shoreline. I am grateful to all of my collaborators for showing me that we can be out of place and better for it. We can trust cycles older than our species. We can do this between-work with grace and surrender. With patience and bravery. With all of who we are. And what made us will reclaim us as soon as the tide.

My love to all of you multiple and hungry, navigating these contrasts of ocean and air. I bow to your impulse to risk the familiar to learn something else and then bring it on home. And most of all, to you who hold home in your hearts for me. Thank you for welcoming me back once more.

The contemporary sperm whale (*Physeter macrocephalus*) has an ancestor with the over-the-top literary name *Livyatan melvillei*. Named backwards after the biblical sea monster and Herman Melville, this ancestor was known for its sharp teeth and massive size. In fact, paleontologists claim they had the largest teeth of any animal ever (excluding tusks)—at over a foot long. Debates are happening on the Internet right now about who would win in a battle between this whale and the ancient Megalodon shark that lived at the same time. They call this whale "raptorial" (look at the root of the word: rape), monstrous, inherently violent.

The name *Livyatan* (the paleontologists wanted to use the spelling "Leviathan," but it was taken so they used the Hebrew spelling) has its own ancestors, derived from Lotan, an Ugaritic name for "the fugitive serpent." As an adjective, the word means "coiled" or "twisted," like the way etymology moves forwards and backwards. Like the way the Leviathan shows up in the Judeo-Christian texts serving multiple functions, the main one being double-edged: what a great god that could create a Leviathan, but especially what a great god that could destroy a Leviathan. As the book of Job tells us, surrender to God. Or as Thomas Hobbes suggests in his book *Leviathan*, surrender and be governed by an absolute sovereign.

I wonder too all the time about creation and destruction. The role of ancestral power. Surrender and change. I wonder what happened over millions of years for a being known for its sharp teeth to evolve into one whose teeth scientists now theorize are never used to chew, but are actually mechanisms that simply attune their echolocation. Is that possible? That what was made to puncture you could now be used to listen deeply? Is the sperm whale diving deep for ancestral elevation? Or was that always the function of their teeth? Did the sea monster stories bias the paleontologists?

The way I look back is influenced by the stories I know now. And I do think that some of my ancestors were monsters. And I do still hold the power to create and destroy, if first in my imagination. And I thought my sharp critique was such a big deal once, how I could use it to cut through the obstacles in my path, to wound the self-righteous. Yes, I aspired to dominate in a world that oppressed me. But now I need antennae for a world I can't imagine. Now I need to listen more than I need to say this. But I do still need to say this:

I surrender. To a love so big it could face and acknowledge monsters. To a love so deep and wide it could create oceans and whales. To an ancestral reach so long it could become us.

And when they name us back what will they say? What stories will they use? How great a love, that could create all this? How will they name all of what we destroyed? What fugitive intentions will survive? Or will the planet sing again without us? I surrender. To a love too big to name.

Tucuxi is a quiet dolphin, the smallest. The international conservationists list the species as "data-deficient," which means they don't know what they don't know, but we knew that. One guess about this dolphin who lives in the estuaries and river basins of Brazil or close to the coast and as far north as Nicaragua, is that she times her cycles to the rising water, conceiving at the peak of the flood when the river out does herself, spills over. And then she nurtures the idea all through the dry season and gives birth when the water is lower and the rain starts again and the fish come back together, easier to find.

What if I could do that? Time the water inside me to the greater cycle of tides, to the memory of flood, to the ebb of my context. What if I could keep nurturing this possibility while the river contracts? Could I cultivate faith that rain will return to my life when I need it? That the resources are gathering somewhere beyond where I swim?

The problem with data-deficiency is that it blocks accountability. It means if they kill you and your sisters in secret, it just stays a secret. It don't look like a pattern. It means that for decades the world will assume you exist, that the work will just happen. But what if there is other information in our own red rivers, our brackish tear ducts, our salted sweat? What if the water remembers us better than the news forgets? I can time my rebirth to the water within you, the flood of your face, the dry of your throat sometimes, the secret you hold. I believe in the flow of your future. I believe in the rain.

Praisesong for the menopausal planet who knows herself well enough to see your nonsense for what it is. Praisesong for she who has known ice ages and asteroids. You will never outsmart her, so you might as well get on her good side.

The striped dolphin could teach us something about this. Acrobatic and swift, even she knows to listen to big mama's breathing, her sweating, her round graceful dance through the days. In the deep water, striped dolphins and their cousins follow where she leads. Like the gulf stream, which is a massive trajectory of warm water (150 times the amount of water in the Amazon River), that flows up out of the Caribbean and is responsible for the palm trees growing on the coasts of South Carolina and Ireland. Or Kuroshio Current in the Pacific, the Agulhas Current near the southern African coast. A study by scholars at the University of Washington, who used sensors at the bottom of the ocean and satellites, says the warm currents are slowing down because of how we have changed the atmosphere. Didn't anyone ever tell you not to mess with a grown woman's radio waves, thermostat, breathing room, or time?

Oh mama. I wish we could be more like striped dolphins, knowing that the patterns of our own bodies are maps to yours, not to be avoided, but to be surrendered to, like flow. I want to tune my movement to where the warmth is, but instead I struggle, treading water on a path I made up in my mind based on bad information. And if I had trusted you, I would have learned to trust myself. And if I had watched you I could have truly seen myself. And I wonder if maybe it's not too late to get off this toxic, white cruise ship and let go control, like Avey in Paule Marshall's *Praisesong for the Widow*.[41]

---

41 Paule Marshall, *Praisesong for the Widow* (New York: Plume, 1983).

Where you are warm, you are wise and you let your warmth flow where it needs to. Where you are cold, you are tight and you let your salt sink to the silt. Any and everywhere you are, you are moving. Vessel for water, holder of space, round revolution. Your cycles make everything. And you let the moon love you and pull on your tears. And you've let us live here long enough to remember. And the length of the lesson is letting us go. We can learn to let go or you will let us go for us. With a rush and a surge and a kiss of renewal. You'll embrace us again. Send us back to the stars.[42]

42 #unendingpraiseforpaulemarshall

For more on menopausal wisdom please do subscribe to Osunfunke Omisade Burney-Scott's brilliant *Black Girls' Guide to Surviving Menopause* podcast.

fifteen

go deep

WHAT DOES IT TAKE TO go deep, below the surface of current events and social media reactions? What would allow you to look at what is under your actions, and under that, and under that? Sperm whales dive a mile deep. Maybe they can give us some advice. And the ocean itself has so many depth lessons, when you think you've reached the bottom, there is sometimes still deeper to go. Take a breath.

A Guide for Diving Deeper

(From cachalot aka *Phyester macrocephalus*, aka the sperm whale who can dive more than a mile deep.)

one. breathe.
(we sperm whales can replace 90 percent of the air in our lungs with one breath. we can blow our breath seventeen feet high. however deep you are breathing, breathe more, exhale longer.)

two. take responsibility for your forehead.
(we, for example, have a head full of wax we can solidify like a weight to go deeper, we can melt it to become lighter than water and float. what is going on in your head? be intentional with it.)

three. hush.
(we stretch out our bodies sixty feet long at the surface and then arch our backs facing down, our tails come with us "barely creating a ripple." we are saving our energy for depth. this is not the time to splash.)

four. be flexible.
(deep in the ocean there is pressure. a lot of pressure. it will press on your chest and your lungs will collapse. you call it heartbreak. it is not. it is how what made you embraces you. reshapes you. welcomes you back. let it happen.)

five. be specific in your actions.
(when your lungs collapse you will need the oxygen in your blood. it is deep in your muscles. it was put there by practice. let your practice facilitate depth. it will be there when you need it.)

six. listen.
(we listen underneath our throats, not with our ears. we listen across the planet. we can hear each other click from opposite sides of the globe. though we may seem alone, we never are.)

seven. come back.
(you will know when it has been enough time in the deep. it can vary. attune to your need. account for your nourishment. direct your thoughts, melt them down make them light. and return.)

Lissodelphis dolphins (called right whale dolphins by single-minded whalers) and many other sea creatures depend on the "deep scattering layer" for their sustenance. What is the deep scattering layer? Is it the point when I am immersed in a project when it somehow seems to fall apart? No. It's cooler than that.

There is a depth of the ocean (300–400 meters deep) that is so thick with life that World War II sonar operators thought it was the bottom of the ocean. But it was not the bottom. It was a bajillion tiny swim bladders reflecting their sonar back to them. *What is a swim bladder?* It's an air-filled organ that fish have, which allows them to ballast, or maintain their depth. (Like what I need when I'm immersed in a project and about to give up.) Did everyone else already know about these things?

False bottoms in the ocean that sound can't travel through? Depth bladders? *Lissodelphis* of the southern and northern hemispheres, thank you for knowing where in the deep there is life thick enough to sustain thousands. Like Jesus underwater you found the thousand fishes, found a floor in the ocean. How divine.

And what about us? How do we stay deep when distracting distractions distract us (like racists being racist for racist reasons)? How do you keep your swim bladder level right so you don't float out of school formation? How do we know the depth at which life is abundant enough to feed us and our families and communities at once? How do you know when the school that you are part of will feed something larger than you? Could a school that thick stop the telescope construction on a sacred Mauna Kea in Hawaii,[43] stop mining in Jamaica's sacred cockpit country,[44] oust a colonial governor in Puerto Rico?[45] Could we be that thick?

Maybe it has to do with the humility of knowing that while we navigate the predictable there are phenomena old and ongoing that we've never even heard about, waiting for us to remember.

What I know is I am proud of you, for the depth of work you are doing, for the layers you are uncovering, for the changes you made when you learned that what you thought was rock bottom was just a reflection of a sound you were making called *need*. For the thickness of your life and who it feeds. For the way you always teach me something new. Generous with all my layered needs.

How diligent your breath for staying deep. And all the noise that bounces off our lives. How powerful we are when we're together. We could confuse the warships, scatter sound. We could change the entire story with what we know. That this is not the bottom, this is life. This is not the floor, this is not even a wall, this is our air.

---

43 Https://earther.gizmodo.com/hundreds-of-protestors-block-work
-crews-ahead-of-thirty-1836443987.

44 Https://youtu.be/RBtwY2lp_cM.

45 Https://www.npr.org/2019/07/18/742957579/puerto-rican-police
-fire-tear-gas-at-huge-protests-over-governors-texts.

sixteen

stay black

THERE ARE SEVERAL PRACTICES OF marine mammals that res-
onate with Black freedom movement strategies and tenden-
cies. And the scientific surveillance and profiling technologies
that describe marine mammals hold much in common with
the systems that criminalize Blackness too. From the young
narwhal as Black Unicorn (in Audre Lorde's sense of the
term), to a whale whose Latin name means "punkinhead" to
the slim Black panther of the ocean to the extinct Caribbean
monk seals, who were the first victims of Columbus and
whose blubber was used to literally lubricate the plantation
infrastructure of the region, this section explores Black kinship with marine mammals and the possibility of solidarity,
love, chosen family, new traditions, and abundant survival.

Black unicorns are real. They are young narwhals. Not every young female-assigned narwhal has a sensitive cone that breathes seawater to measure and break through her surroundings, but some do. Enough do that I think the myth that only male narwhals have horns is more about how scientists think about the phallus than about the lives of our unicorn teachers in the Arctic.

Audre Lorde already told us:

> The black unicorn was mistaken
> for a shadow
> or symbol
> and taken
> through a cold country
> where mist painted mockeries
> of my fury.[46]

Over time, the young narwhal will look more like the ice that surrounds her, but right now she is Black like the depth from whence she came. She is sharp as she needs to be and determined to breathe even in frozen places. Not every Black unicorn is showing you her horn. But some of us are here reorganizing your daydreams. You are welcome.

How I love us, Black unicorns, I love the youth of our adaptation. I love every way our bodies tell us not to blend in to what surrounds us, but instead to break through with brave sensitivity. Though we are hunted for exactly what makes us strong, may we always be embraced in the words of the Lorde. May we ever attune ourselves and support each other in this breakthrough. I have always believed in us.

---

46 See Audre Lorde, "The Black Unicorn," in *The Black Unicorn* (New York: W.W. Norton, 1978), 3.

I love the layered Blackness of the Melon-headed whale, *Peponocephala electra* (whose Latin name translates to "punkinhead"). Black and then more Black. Black with masks of Black across her Blackness. Black in the way that Toni Morrison's Pilate describes it, "may as well be a rainbow."[47]

Punkinhead, the pantropical, has long been known by her associations with certain dolphins, yes Sawarak and them, the rough-toothed also. At a distance the only way to tell her apart from a pygmy killer whale—also known as slender Blackfish, not to be confused with Punkinhead herself, who went by many-toothed Blackfish, and of course not to be confused with the actual orca, the Blackfish of Blackfish who everybody knows is part white on both sides... The only way to tell Punkinhead apart from Slim at a distance is to note who she's rolling with. Her associations are powerful.

In fact, in the first report of interspecies cetacean adoption in the open ocean, a lost melon-headed whale adopted a pod of common bottlenose dolphins. A mother, a sister, and the whole family. The adoptive mother has been attentive and nurturing. The adoptive sister has been appropriately annoyed. Punkinhead studied the behaviors of this new family and rather quickly learned the line dances and their particular rules for spades. Who knows? Maybe next year Punkinhead will bring the potato salad to the cookout, or the rice and peas to the boat race, or the fufu to the village wedding, the roti for... What was I saying? Y'all hungry?

Oh yes. I love the way you live a layered Blackness where Black meets Black across itself as Black. How you make family out of need and tradition out of what is left and found. Praise the technology of play-cousins and sister-friends.

---

47 See Toni Morrison, *Song of Solomon* (New York: Knopf, 1977).

Praise the sweet way the mundane becomes sacred in your hands. How a spade becomes a spade by digging in. How freedom becomes fertile because we insist we can be socially alive on top of everything. May as well be a carnival, an eastern parkway parade, the Shinnecock Labor Day powwow as well. I'll see you there, as well, as depth as deep as wellness, as wide as grace as Black as love. May as well be. May as well be a rainbow.

So Punkinhead, *Peponacephala electra*, known by many names, travels in a Black collective. Close. The many-toothed Blackfish move by the hundreds across the planet, organized and committed to each other. If they strand, they strand together. If they don't strand, they are difficult to track. The way they move, tight-knit and massive, means scientists struggle to get a good view of them, confusing them often with other Black dolphins and whales. You can distinguish them by their associations with certain dolphins (spinner, Sarawak). Pantropically associated, they are sometimes called the electra dolphin, sometimes called the little killer whale. (Their scientific name is a Latin lab mistranslation from the sixties, that literally means punkinhead. Like many embarrassing nicknames, it stuck.)

This is what they do. They rest in the morning, from sunrise to noon. They breathe on the surface, then wake. All afternoon they whistle to each other at a frequency mostly beyond our hearing range, past the limits of the recording devices of bioacoustic researchers.[48] And at night, when Black

---

48 A recording of their afternoon sounds (the background sounds to me like an old Black Carolina church congregational hymn) can be found at https://vimeo.com/304611272.

is Black as they are Black, they work. They forage for food, moving massive unseen. They find what's at the bottom, they click echolocate, eat by shape. They know the shape of themselves and the shape of what they need. Or you could say their Black work of collective nurturance happens in a Black context, in the open ocean, all night long. Supported by the darkness. And when the sun comes up they rest again.

I wonder what you know about close. About Black. About making the wrong decision all together at the same time. About moving not by sight but by communion. About whole mornings of breathing and afternoons of congregation. About collective Black movement and the effective cloak of splash. About the nourishment of dark. The click of knowing.

Yes. I would breathe all morning, rest the sunrise into heat. Yes. I would wake up and listen for your call. I would whistle at a frequency more for feeling than for hearing. I would sing with you the whole rest of the day. And when it is time, in these dark hours at the depth of what we've done, I can hear you. I can feel you. We'll find everything we need.

And then there's Slim. Sometimes they say Punkinhead (the melon-headed whale) or another Blackfish fits the description, but only Slim is Slim. The slender Blackfish, *Feresa attenuata*, they say that Slim is a killer. Alias pygmy killer whale. More killer than the actual killer whale to hear them tell it.

The Audubon guide calls them "pugnacious." Twice. I heard they tried to lock Slim up and it was bad news for

---

A description of their sounds by bioacoustic researchers off Hawaii, can be found at https://asa.scitation.org/doi/10.1121/1.3365259.

everyone involved, trainers, cellmates. Slim refuses to be caged. Yup. Slim will cut you.

Sleek and not easily surveilled. The guidebooks say Slim is rarely seen, but could be almost anywhere. They think that Slim's avoiding boats on purpose. And so Slim's reputation continues to grow, while her sacred practices like birth, love, and communion stay out of view.

And maybe it's my own soft spot for the Black and hard to place. Maybe it's daddy issues, who knows? But I like to think of Slim as a guardian, not a criminal. I like to think of Slim's stealth as protective of a greater work than Babylon can bear. Whereas other whales click or sing, they say that Slim is growling at the surface. The ocean's own Black Panther. They say Slim doesn't leap and flip like other dolphins. They "seem slow and lethargic," the *Audubon* laments, in comparison to the other funner dolphins that play with boats.

Slim is not lazy. Slim is coolly calm. And all because Slim did not come to play.

Pantropical protector, what would make us worthy of you? As the Amazon Rainforest, the lungs of Earth burn and politicians do nothing. As the real killers pollute the ocean and poison their own futures. And you protect your whole process from us. You didn't need permission to be so gorgeous and untraceable, uncageable, untrappable. You slide out of your name to code and alias.

Who criminalize you for exceeding the terms of a deadly contract. Who call you killer for refusing to perform for killers. Who cannot find you and yet seeks to name you small. Who call you out your name don't know what I know. Don't want what I want. Which is pantropical peace and freedom.

Which is for those who deny their own violence to fear me. To imagine I could be anywhere unseen. To teach themselves how Black and free the world is. How total and slippery love is. How hungry and persistent life is. Until no one needs to sweat you. Burn up paper-chasing what you already have. Which is breath and depth and your own life. Which is stealth and specificity, your own terms. Which is what the planet is, quiet as its kept. None of our business.

Once upon a time, whiteness protected baby harp seals from predators. It helped them blend into the snow. No one could see them. But hundreds of years ago whiteness turned against them, when humans gave whiteness another meaning. Operationalized that whiteness for money and coats. Maybe they learned something new—harp seals of that time—about what a predator would do with the technology of whiteness.

Thank goodness harp seals know how to let it go. They stay white for a couple of weeks and then shed all that mess. Poof. For a layered existence. What would a harp seal look like, trying to stay immature, never learning to swim, living only at the surface. No, that wouldn't be helpful at all. Especially if, for example, you melted Earth.

Once upon a time there was whiteness. It will soon be a memory. Are you learning to swim?

And my love to those of us who have always stood out stark against surface whiteness and therefore dug deep down and dove. Thank goodness we learned how to breathe. Remembering a depth before all of this. That lives on.

Though they outlawed the international trade in our bodies, it is still legal to hunt us. The winged whale with the sharp snout (*Balaenoptera acutorostrata*) is the smallest baleen whale, and also the only one it's still legal to hunt commercially.

Not surprisingly the guidebooks describe the hunted as the haunting. This whale they say, "may suddenly appear alongside you without warning" and "may vanish without a trace." If you study the movements of the hunted (which is exactly what hunters do), you will notice patterns. The dive pattern of the sharp-winged is distinctive, they say. They emerge out of the water at a forty-five degree angle, they don't show their tails. When they travel in groups, those groups are self-segregated by sex, age, and reproductive condition. No one knows where they are actually born, but sound recordings suggest that maybe they give birth in the deep water surrounding the lesser Antilles, the small islands where some of my people are from. They say you can't see them breathing, but you can hear them "on a calm day."

Sometimes they identify us by our lack of scars. Many times they have just watched, took notes while orcas attacked us. Though they couldn't find where we were from, nor accurately count how many of us existed, they said it was legal to hunt us. Because, though we were small, we were large, and in their imaginations there must have been many of us. And though we were here, we were there, though we were sharp we had wings, and what we were doing with our tails, we must have fit the description.

All my love to the hunted, the traded, the betrayed. All my love to the haunting, the disciplined, the discrete. I know what it is to be somebody's nightmare all day. But when I dream you, you are free. And your wings are unhidden and your sharp face relaxes and you breathe when you want to and loud. When you want to and how. And no one can catch you.

The scientific community believes that the Caribbean monk seal is extinct. The last verified sighting was in 1952, a couple of years before my father was born. Turns out, one of the very first things Columbus and them did when they got to the Caribbean was to kill monk seals. Six of them. Immediately upon arrival. They say the Caribbean monk seal, born Black and proud, was never afraid of the colonizers. And, in fact, they remained curious and calm. And the colonizers continued to use their own methods, which were fear-based and not calm at all. And genocidal.

The oil in the blubber of Caribbean monk seals literally lubricated the machinery of the plantation economy. Without it nothing could function. It is said that some plantations in the Caribbean required hunts for monk seals every single night, so that the machinery for processing sugar cane could be smooth the next day.

I cannot say that my father was a Caribbean monk, though there were a few transplanted and held in the New York Aquarium before he was born. They believe that, by the time the Caribbean monk seal was placed on the endangered species list, it was already extinct. I cannot say that Clyde Gumbs, who died of prostate cancer, diagnosed too late, was a Caribbean monk. I cannot say he was a monk at all. I can only say he had very few earthly possessions. And he wore the same outfit every day. I can say, yes, he had habits and rituals. I can say, when he lived in the Caribbean, he observed the sunrise and the sunset every morning and evening, squinting through a small digital camera. I can say, yes, he was curious and calm. And some people took advantage. I can say he was born Black, but I cannot say that he was never afraid. What he died from, the opposite of a healthcare system, a machine that turns Black death into sugar. Yes. I can say it is genocidal.

Sometimes, usually in Haiti and Jamaica, people swear they see a Caribbean monk. The scientific community believes this is impossible, saying they are probably hooded seals out of range. But if you happen, by some miracle, to see him, will you tell him I say thank you for being Black and curious? Thank you for being calm and brave. And that I honor you for continuing to be who you were, no matter what they tried to turn you into, despite their hunting every night. And say I love you with a sweetness, not of sugar but of salt that won't dissolve. I love you with a Black outliving empires in your name. Sun rise. Sun set.

seventeen

slow down

WHERE DO YOU THINK YOU are going so fast? This section offers slowing down as a strategic intervention in a world on speed, and an appropriate response to the exact urgencies that make us feel we cannot slow down. It is the speed, the speed-boats, the momentum of capitalism, the expediency of pollution that threatens the ocean, our marine mammal mentors, and our own lives. What if we could release ourselves from an internalized time clock and remember that slow is efficient, slow is effective, slow is beautiful?

Before she goes underwater, the harbor seal will slow her heart. Yes. From 120 beats per minute to three or four heartbeats. Per minute.

But first she exhales.

When she is underwater, the oxygen she needs is the oxygen she has. Her blood breathes for her through her muscles as she descends as deep as 1,500 feet. Deep enough for what she needs to do. She slows her heart and listens, reaches, knows.

What if you could hear the world between your heartbeats? Slow down enough to deepen into trust. How can I learn the skill to tell my heart slow down? The pressure is coming. Slow down and we will have the air we need. Slow down and trust the ocean underneath you. And live in it, the underneath that nourishes love, your blubbered warmth, your sleek survival, you among the most abundant seals.

And then you come back. Out to the surface and you race your heart to meet the sky, you breathe again to feel the world. Your heart. The speed of recognition. Your heart. The waking of your lungs.

I love you so much, that I would learn my changing heart.

The way it slows and when it quickens. The space between, and all this closeness. I would breathe at the pace that love requires. Which is not always the same, but is always here. My heart.

The harbor seal lives half her life in water. Half her life on land. And through it all, she has to know her heart, what it makes possible. Her breath and what it needs.

And I can live this whole life from my heart. Despite all my impatience and my fear. I can know my heart, like love knows you. Has always known. Ready? Exhale.

The Amazonian manatee has no nails. Her teeth are round for eating plants. They rotate and replace themselves. Her only protection is home. The dark fresh water of the Amazon River Basin, the forest when it floods. Mostly they don't know what she is doing when she's free. What impacts her well-being the most? Water. Levels of water. Where water flows. Water is home.

The Amazonian manatee lives in the Amazon. Not a safe place to try to be at home. Her habitat, and that of every animal and plant of the great Amazon region is under constant threat. Commercial interests have cut and blazed and burned so much of the Amazon away. In 2019, massive fires burned through the Amazon and the response was slow and stubborn. Lying politicians like Bolsonaro blamed environmentalists for the fires and dragged their feet to respond. This is the water you would use if you were trying to fight a fire, the water where the Amazonian manatee lives. And these fires blazed through August when water levels were lowering.

And consider the history of the Amazonian manatee, who, like her home, is sacrificed for commerce. Not only does she have less space to be at home. They hunt her body. Harpoon her peace. Once upon a time (1935–1954) her flesh and skin were major exports for Brazil. And her families, once large, have become small because of that. Reports say that even though the Amazonian manatee is "protected" in her entire range, she is still hunted to provide meat for the military. That same military that will not protect the Amazonian lungs of the Earth. That same military that at best stands by amidst assassinations of the activists, especially Black and Indigenous, activists and visionaries who oppose the corporate harm of the local environment and the exploitation of their people. The Amazon region. Not a safe place to try to be at home.

What has the Amazonian manatee learned in all this time? They say she is the most social manatee in the world, she without nails. Not only nurturing mother–calf bonds but traveling in families of about ten now—used to be larger.

They say she don't study day or night, just water and where is it, and how much of it is there and what is it nurturing, what now grows. And in the dry season, they say she has reserves. Fat is a winning strategy. She can go two hundred days without eating. A floating hibernation. She has learned to wait for water. She may be ready for how long it takes for us to remember the conditions of our breathing. Can she wait for us to stop selling our children out from under us? Can she wait for us to stop selling the air out of our lungs? Can she wait for us to learn to be at home?

I don't know. What I do know is water. And how it rises to the surface when I think of you. Water and how it floods me when I know. Water and what it means and what it could do and how we need it. In a world on fire where we are called to grow.

From some angles, you might mistake me for a stone. I have tusks but you will not see them until I want you to see them. It was me. I mowed the sea grass, left crop circle maps to underwater cities. And when you disturbed my days with greed, then I switched up. Became nocturnal. I move slowly but consistently and travel a thousand miles. Sometimes, to breathe, I stand up on my tail. Do you yet know me? Scientists say they do not know why sometimes hundreds of us gather. And I'm not telling.

With a tail like a whale and a body like a manatee, dugong is the closest living relative of the extinct *Hydrodamalis gigas*. All along the coasts of East Africa, Asia, and Australia, the only members of the order *sirenia* (the original merfolk) in the Indian and Pacific oceans, dugong is now the star of tourist adventures. There are conflicting reports on their mating rituals. In some areas, the female-assigned dugongs attract a group of male assigned. In some areas, the male-assigned du-gongs display themselves to attract the female assigned. And who knows about all the attractions scientists haven't learned to watch for or categorize? And the big parties that seem not to serve a reproductive or nutritious function? Maybe attraction is something different than you thought. Maybe it matters where we are. Maybe you don't know what we want.

From some angles, you might mistake me for a stone, breathing steady through the shallow places. The cow they say, the camel of the sea. What will you learn? Patience and diligence, when to stand, how to rearrange your life when conditions change? That would be useful.

I love you as you change. I love you slowly moving through. I love the tusks I cannot see. I love the way you love your love for your own reasons. Sometimes when you love the coast enough you become shoreline. Move so steady on the floor algae grows on you. Sometimes the way you love is perfectly on time and very slow is fast enough. So keep on breathing.

eighteen

rest

AND SO THERE IS TIME to rest, like sea elephants who spend
a whole month just snuggling and shedding their skin, pusa
seals who dive deeper postpartum and spend more time
alone, gray seals who offer a third of their bodyweight while
nursing and then leave to regenerate themselves. This section
argues the urgency of rest, the necessity of regeneration, and
the depth rest reveals and allows.

A mother gray seal loses thirteen pounds a day while nursing. That would mean, in the three or four weeks before weaning and mating again, she will lose 83 percent of her bodyweight. The maximum measured weight of a female-assigned gray seal is 440 lbs. Thirteen pounds is a third of the weight of the pup itself at birth (29–40 lbs.). In those three or four weeks, the pup will triple or quadruple in size.

She does take breaks to eat though. Occasionally she takes a break to eat. Those last about 1–3 minutes, including the time it takes to dive down to the seafloor and come back.

Is this a word problem? I think about the proportional cost of intimate creation. How much it takes. What we give to the world we are growing. Where we give it from and how we maintain. I am stunned by the math.

But maybe it *is* a word problem. I have learned the phrase "give it her all." I have heard people praised over and over again as "tireless," right through their exhaustion and death. I myself have forgotten to eat.

What if we made the calculation? Thirteen lbs. a day and only minutes to replenish. An offering so huge we barely exist. A dive we have to make and come right back. Just the simple awareness of how much of myself is swimming away now. How much I offer that I'll never hold. And I must be made new, because I gave you my all. And I must be my all, because you must be made, new.

And sometimes a gray seal will stay out twenty whole days in the sea remembering those thin minute weeks, what it took and will take. And if I say my love is a renewable resource, then that would mean that my renewal is love. My renewal is sacred. My renewal is everything. My renewal is you. Your whole body is made from it actually. But who's counting?

Postpartum, pusa seals dive ten times as deep as ever. They stay there in the depth for twice or even six times as long. No one knows what they are doing. Some theorize they may be resting. And why not? After a birth that they prepared for by building multi-room dwellings under the ice to keep the family safe from polar bears and humans, so life could emerge. Why not? All I know is that the depth of the hunted creatrix cannot be known in shallow terms. And we deserve space to reflect on what we made.

Love to you builders of worlds that no one sees. Love to you makers of life beyond our view. Love to you, and gratitude for all the depth it takes for you to do the private work, the deepest dive of loving you.

The *miouroung*, or southern sea elephants, spend a whole month snuggling. This is after breeding season is already over and done. Just a platonic month of spooning with relatives and friends. They press right up onto each other on the beach and mostly nap. And this is all they do for an entire month. No hunting, mating, or territory struggles, just snuggling like a full-time job. And during this time they shed their skin. They become silver and new. At the end of the month, they will swim off one by one and spend most of their time 2,000 feet underwater eating, but for now all there is to do is sleep off who we were.

There are layers of myself I need to shed now. And rest is the only way to be renewed. One month of summer I'll be home, becoming something iridescent, vulnerable, older and new.

And you?

Thank you for all the forms of intimacy that teach me what my skin is not and what my armor never was. I wish for you the sacredness of rest, expansive sprawling rest un-interrupted. I love the part of you that is emerging under everything. You deserve to rest long enough to let whatever go. I put my skin right next to yours to let you know that even when you seem alone, I'm with you. And I will wait to see the silver next of you, before you dive again.

nineteen

take care of your blessings

THE BLACK FEMINIST AUTHOR (AND pleasure activism ancestor!) Toni Cade Bambara used to sign her emails "Take Care
of your Blessings," an acronym of her initials, TCB. This
section looks at the revolutionary parenting and commu-
nity-care practices modeled by marine mammals. Consider
singing seals, who use delayed implantation to give birth
when and where they want life to enter or marine otters who
make their bodies into rafts for their children. Note crabeater
seals, who organize themselves to protect parent–child bond-
ing, and the range of what scientists call the allomaternal
behavior of marine mammals that adopt each other beyond
birth relation or even species. The question is, how can we
best care for each other across generations, borders, and other
barriers? Or as Audre Lorde said, "we must be very strong/
and love each other/ in order to go on living."[49]

---

49 Audre Lorde, "Equinox" in *From A Land Where Other People Live*
(Detroit: Broadside Press, 1973), 11–12.

Lutra felina, the marine otter, lives on the rockiest shoreline with the roughest of waves. She keeps secrets. Like how long she will live, what she does at night. She has not let you measure her children. I think she is smart, this cat of the ocean. The guidebooks say she is secretive, but I wonder if you are just scared to go where she lives, where the rocks are so sharp and the waves beat the shoreline.

They say sometimes she screams a high-pitched scream. Swims usually with her head barely out of the water.

Sometimes she floats on her back, makes herself into a raft for her babies, usually twins, sometimes triplets, quadruplets. She lives in a hard place and in between rocks. She puts her back to the future and her face to her children. I think she is smart to take care of her secrets. When you live in a hard place, precious cargo on your chest. When you say with your whiskers and claws "do not go there," there should be some respect.

And I offer my love to your nails and your secrets, your teeth and technology, your heaviness of hair, your float and your leap. I can hardly believe that the waves did not break you. And your scream? It is scripture and wall. It is map. And you teach me to keep my treasures on my heart where I can feel them. And to keep my eyes on them too. And my body a boat balanced starboard and port. And my face facing aft after float. And my scream too a scripture as sacred as love. And my choice.

Sing the shape of the singing seal (*Ommatophoca rossii*) named after a sea named after a seaman who colonized her body and the place she lives, all under his name. (Ross. An unfair bargain.)

Sing her shape. She who yet sings open-mouthed or between her teeth or in her growing chest, her expanding throat.

She shapes her body up like "s," like yes like snake like siren song. The rarest smallest seal of sharpened teeth and biggest eyes is wise enough to tempt the frozen air.

They say, when the singing seal is threatened, she sings inside her throat a trill, a chug, a lock, beatboxes till you turn away. But then some others say they cannot tell. When she opens her mouth, arches her neck is it aggressive or submissive? Is it fighting stance or friendship? Who's to say? The singing seal is rarely seen and usually alone. It took a while to figure out how they mate at all. Like some other seals, she can hold her pregnancy like a secret, delaying implantation until she finds the right place, the right time, the worthy ice. So gestation is nine months, but not from conception, from implantation. Something happens deep inside her when no one else is around. Something only she knows happens when she's ready and not before.

Me too. Maybe you don't know if I am singing or screaming sometimes. Maybe you don't know if I want you to stay or leave. Maybe I hold my secrets deep within on my own time, and use my oversized eyes to dive so deep you cannot see. So you don't. See me. It is something, living on pack ice and eating squid from the bottom of the ocean. And then coming up into cold air to sing. There is something that I need, but I have to go so deep to find it. There is something I have to give, but I have to give it on my own time. There is something I'm going to tell you, but first I have to make a language for myself and the place I live that doesn't steal me from my purpose. Will you wait? There is something I'm going to tell you, just let me open up my mouth. See if I sing.

Arctocephalus gazella, hunted under the name Antarctic fur seal spends most of her time alone. She has already survived the end of the world. Her species was killed by the millions for fur, but a few ancestors remained on Bird Island, and regenerated towards the current population. What does she know? She is mostly at sea, gathering with her kin back to the land she was born on only to give birth again. Even when she is nursing, she leaves her pup for up to two weeks at a time to find food and then comes back to feed her for a couple of days and then leaves. She comes back until the pup can swim out too. Her mothering is shaped by the imperative to regenerate herself at a distance.

If you are interested in the poetics, the scientists call this "income breeding," meaning she has to go find and eat enough food to be able to lactate, as distinct from "capital breeding," which some other seals do, feeding from stores they have already accumulated. The British Antarctic Survey measures her absence with VHF tags. When she is on land, the sensor works. They hear her. When she is out at sea they can't hear a thing. In krill-abundant years, she may come back after a day or so, but sometimes she has to go further and further out to find enough income to bring something back. And then give it all away. And then go back out again. We know something about this in my family.

I am writing this on World Oceans Day. The whole world is an ocean. Everyday belongs to salt, the world you retain and hunger for. Thank you island ancestors for going out to sea, regenerating the slim possibility that we could exist. Thank you mamas for going as far as you went, as far as you needed to, and for what you brought back. I could plot point the absence with charts and sharp angles, but gratitude is immeasurably round. For every time you remade yourself in the face of necessity, for the whole salt world in your tears, for every time you gave me what you found and let me grow with it. What I know is that distance has grown me. And I can be with the ocean of myself. And I can do the untrackable work they don't see, what it takes to come back home to you.

Love ice. Not war. Walruses of any sex assignment can have tusks as long as a meter. The dominant theory is that the main use of these tusks is male struggles for dominance. But I'm not convinced. Especially since tusks are not sex-specific. And walruses regularly use these extended front teeth to perform miracles, like pulling their up to 4,200 pound bodies onto ice.

Mother walruses use their tusks to protect their calves and to carve out two and a half years of intimate feeding, more than most mammals in the Arctic can afford (and despite the fact that newborn walruses can dive for food almost immediately). Notably, sometimes walruses use their tusks to puncture inflatable research boats. In 2019, they sunk a Russian Navy ship. And they have actually done a very good job of retaining their reproductive privacy as a species.

Until recently, scientists didn't know much about walrus reproductive behavior. They still don't know why they seem to wait years after reproductive maturity to actually reproduce. They have watched a mating ritual among Pacific walruses where walruses sing their partners into the water to mate. Maybe they are waiting until they can produce or decipher a worthy song. Who knows?

I haven't seen scientists admit that these centuries of reproductive privacy are because of a fear of tusks. They say it is because of walrus's love for ice. "Because of the ice-loving, or pagophilic habits, of the Walrus, scientists know relatively little about its breeding behavior." As the planet melts, researchers have more access to walrus observation in their intimate moments. And of course walruses have less safe places to live. Like other people in the time of global heat. On a hot day, a walrus will turn bright pink to thermoregulate with blood. And as the oceans rise, what will we learn?

Pagophilic. To love ice on a melting planet. To cherish ice for your own reasons. To trust ice to provide sanctuary. To need ice as a barrier between you and a species of people, a segment of which would create something that destroys families, seeks to eradicate sanctuary, violates privacy and home, and call it ICE. We have so much to learn from the walrus. But we could do some of it by looking at ourselves.

What if sanctuary is a form of love that respects your organic boundaries? Abides with the distance your intimacy needs? Respects the song of your own time? Your growth? Because I admire your teeth and where they brought you, and what they lifted, and who you protected, and what you evaded and what you know. And I love you where you are. I love you where you need to be. My love does not build a wall while breaking your door. My love is patient and thick. It is singing and waiting. And my whole body alarms with the heat of this pressure. It is our blood at the surface. It is fear at the door. It is our evolution of tooth and sound and breathing while the planet floods us home.

Whereas most seals lurch on land, *Lobodon carcinophaga* glides. The crabeater seal (a better description would be the "krilleater seal") travels thousands of miles gracefully, and has been found 3,600 feet above sea level. I mean to say, she goes where she wants. The only large animal on Earth with a bigger population than this seal is you.

She has the most complicated and evolved set of teeth on the planet, lobed interlocking teeth inside her cheeks that filter krill so she can gulp like a whale, taking in only what she needs. Could I be that graceful? To swim on land as well as I do in water? To trust my mouth to specify my needs?

Crabeater seal families nourish and protect each other. A baby seal gains up to 175 pounds in the three weeks that they are nursing. A male-assigned seal (not the biological father) plays a lookout role, while all this fat transfer of life happens. They remain, on the lookout for leopard seals who would love to eat a crabeater seal pup before she grows too quick to catch, too sure to swallow. Researchers note that this role of having a mother's back may be just as important as mating itself, may be exactly the adaptation that makes this seal the most abundant on Earth. Could we be that diligent? Could we remember that protecting each other is our only future? Especially here where we protect each other not on ice, but from ICE?

The crabeater seal is good at being alive, graceful on the move, writing infinity signs on the ice like a message. I think they'll outlast us. But maybe we can evolve our mouths in the shape of need, train our movements for multiple contexts, nurture abundantly, and protect those who nurture. Maybe it's not too late to cultivate grace.

In case, remember I love you. Your mouth that you are still learning to operate. Your body that wants to swim on land and walk on water. Your deep impulse to give. Your imperative to protect the work of feeding generations. Honor it. I strive to honor you. The way you slide on through resilient magic. The spell of your abundant impossibility. Your entire body writes our future infinite. Your breathing body spells our future name.

Much threatens the life of the South American fur seal. Born Black on a rocky shoreline, vampire bats want their blood, sea lions want their babies, oil spills kill them by the thousands, global warming has decimated them already, and that's before mentioning that they have been consistently commercially hunted by humans since 1515, which may be the longest lasting commercial harvest of any seal. And on top of that, they get caught up in nets, and are illegally hunted to decrease competition for commercial fishers. Punished, in other words, for how good they are at feeding their families.

Can you tell I'm not in a great mood? Long of ear, and listening frantically. Threatened by everything. And it's not fair. If it's not the weather, it's pollution. If I avoid the sea lion in the water, there is still the bat in the sky. Should my livelihood depend on fur staying out of style? I didn't ask to be this beautiful.

Sometimes I really feel like the world is against me. Skins me, drowns me, takes my blood, trashes my home. And blames me for being too threateningly brilliant and resourceful at the same time. And I don't know what to do with my rage but dive into it. Dive under it. And try to see what's at the bottom here. 560 feet into the ocean. I can stay underwater for about seven minutes and then I have to breathe. At the bottom of this I just want to be loved, to be heard, to be more than a meal, or a coat, or collateral lost in your mess.

How do I cultivate it, what I actually want, which is to be more than attractive, more than useful, because beauty and use and skill are deadly in the time of extraction? But I also don't want to be expendable to you. Is there any way that I don't lose?

The answer is no.

Maybe I have to nurture something more visceral than sale or security. Maybe I have to clarify my values. While some seals only nurse their children for a few days, the South American fur seal nurses for up to an entire year (the only seal who nurses longer is the nearby Galapagos fur seal, who may nurse for even two or three years). She goes out to feed and returns, finding her loved one by sound, by smell, by promise. And every time she leaves, she knows the reality of sea lions and vampire bats. Next time she comes back there may be no answer, the beach may not smell right. That's the risk of love. You might train your senses to sense a body and return to a world that makes no sense anymore. Can I do that, in a threatening world that's threatened by me? Can I offer fully what would be taken somehow anyway? Can I also risk my heart?

I guess I have to. Otherwise there's only slick water and bad weather, bloodsuckers and booby traps. And I love you with a love that claims all my senses. You are why I grew ears and I'm listening. You are what I would smell, so I breathe.

The West Indian manatee has teeth that move, a migrating set of molars in her mouth that she replaces after use. The West Indian manatee has nails, so do her West African cousins. The West Indian manatee, like all manatees, knows how to move between salt and fresh water in search of warmth, hydration, and vegetation.

The algae blooms of the toxic red tide are a natural threat to the West Indian manatee. Do you know about this? About how, in volatile circumstances, after a storm for example, when the bottom of the ocean has been shaken up considerably, there emerge toxic organisms that spread. If ingested, this red situation interrupts the neural pathways, it can cause very strange behavior, it is deadly on a mass scale. Oh, I'm afraid you do know about this. I feel you trying now to breathe, and wondering about how toxic and contagious these circumstances are, how safe to breathe in volatile conditions like these.

Red tides seem to occur naturally, but some say that human industrial pollution has made them more frequent, toxicity feeds the toxic, amplifies their deadly effect.

So what is a West Indian manatee mother to do in a world like this, of red tide and pollution? A world in which 82 percent of West Indian manatees are killed by humans with fast machines they feel they have a right to. Where death by watercraft collision and death by the simple act of breathing are now common?

Well, sometimes when threatened by humans in masks, a manatee mother will place her body between her child and the threat. Yes. If she has to. More often, they will flee together, mother and child communicating all the while. In a code red situation the mother is speaking, continually teaching, the child is consistently responding, here I am.

Last year, environmentalists said that the West Indian manatee, especially the subspecies in and around Florida, was one of the top two species most threatened by the current federal administration. With the watercraft deaths, a major red tide, and an administration committed to deregulating the few protected areas, the Endangered Species Coalition says it's not a good time to be a manatee (*Miami New Times*).

But I think maybe it is a good time to be a manatee. Manatees are graceful and loving. They can "traverse deep ocean passages." And maybe they can teach us to traverse this. They love to touch each other and wrestle and play underwater. They want to protect each other and be safe. They want to hear each other and be heard. They want to move slow in a world where hurt can escalate so quickly. And they do have teeth that migrate after vegetarian labor. They do have rounded nails on the edges of their flippers.

For your sake, for our sake, I wish there was no such thing as code red. I wish this toxic situation didn't explode and kill so frequently, publicly, unpredictably. Or is it really unpredictable, this red that makes it so hard to breathe today, so many days?

Two things research contends about red tides.

1. you can feed it. toxic pollutants nourish naturally occurring toxins.
2. when they occur, it is because of a stirring up of what was already at the bottom of this context.

Which is to say, this is what it looks like when a context built on violence, fed by toxic garbage every day, blooms to the surface. This is exactly what would bloom here in the wake of genocide, and planted blood, bloody plantations, red lining, and red light criminalization.

The tide is code red when it stops speaking in code.

Could we communicate more like manatees, who stay in communication in all kinds of emergencies, place their bodies in a way that protects children, touch each other to remember and know? Researchers say manatees communicate vocally, and by touch and by taste and by coordinating their breathing and by resting together. I can feel how long we've wanted this, a world where we can hear each other, protect each other, play and touch each other safely, nourish each other generously. Move when we need to move through fresh and salted water, traverse deep ocean passages, get through this place we are, where it's so difficult to breathe.

I can feel it like I feel these wisdom molars moving in my head, my bones, your bones expanding our call and our response. I love you with where I put my body and with how I round my nails and with everything I say. I love you enough to detoxify my blood and eat my vegetables. To look at the bottom of myself for the danger there. I love you enough to respond to your urgent crucial call. Decoded so you hear exactly what I am saying. I love you. I'm here. Come with me. I hear you. I love you. I'm here. Stay with me. Take care.

In 2016, *Scientific Reports* (an arm of *Nature* magazine), published a study about Indo-Pacific dolphin othermothering, foster parenting and adoption or what they call "allomaternal behavior."[50] This is not rare. As the authors of the study point out, mothering by other-than-gestational mothers happens in "every major mammalian taxon." It is that crucial. The adoptive dolphin mother they studied also lactated to feed the calf, whose gestational mother had died. Why, the authors of the study wonder, do mammals do this when, as they put it, "the behavior is costly?" To them, "it is unclear why an animal would invest its resources in this manner."

Does it seem unclear to you?

Who here has not been mothered by someone genetically and socially distant from your birth situation, at some necessary time? And if you have ever shared something, taught someone, shared responsibility for someone's wellness for even a part of their journey, how would you measure what you gained from that potentially "costly behavior?" We call it love.

And the so-called interpersonal is as political as the interspecies. At the 1979 Conference of Third World Lesbians and Gays, Audre Lorde spoke in her keynote address of "our children." And the Third World Lesbian caucus at the conference made it more explicit in their statement, "All third world lesbians share in the responsibility for the care and nurturing of the children of individual lesbians of color." Around the same time, the Sisterhood of Black Single Mothers in Brooklyn promoted and celebrated what they called "motherful" family systems. And many mammals model what we call "revolutionary mothering"—not only feminists of color and dolphins off the coast of Japan.

I see you. And I celebrate your animal investments. Your keen adaptation. Your offerings of faith. Your mothering in moments, months, and over lifetimes. You don't know how it is coming back to you. You know much better than all that.

---

50 M. Sakai, Y. Kita, K. Kogi, et al., "A wild Indo-Pacific bottlenose dolphin adopts a socially and genetically distant neonate," *Scientific Reports* 6 (2016), https://www.nature.com/articles/srep23902.

You simply want us to exist. And love is lifeforce. (Thanks June Jordan!)[51]

Thank you for loving me to excess. Thank you for being willing to "waste" so much time in all this wonder. And for those who wake the wild, the mothering willing worthwhile child in me, as well: you'll never know how great the gift, how deep the well, how well you mammal me.

Give thanks.

51 June Jordan, "The Creative Spirit and Children's Literature" in *Revolutionary Mothering: Love on the Front Lines*, edited by Mai'a Williams, China Martens, and Alexis Pauline Gumbs (Oakland: PM Press, 2016).

twenty

activities

Activities (Solo Version):

Listen:
Record yourself reading one or more of these meditations. Play the sound of your own voice reading the passage(s), or a video of you signing in ASL at different times of the day. What do you notice? What is different about what you notice when you engage the recording first thing in the morning as opposed to before you go to bed, at mid-day, etc.?

Breathe:
Track your breath. A deep intimacy with the breath is crucial for all marine mammals. Use these passages as a measure. Read aloud and see how far you get with one breath. Try this at different times of day and notice if there are any differences in your breathing based on time of day, or based on the subject matter of the passage.

Remember:
Choose a mantra. There may be a short phrase or a sentence in this text that contains something that you need

to remember for this part of your journey. Start with one. Memorize it as a mantra and repeat it to yourself as a meditation. Start with saying it at least ten times in one sitting. You can expand your use of the mantra by saying it once a day, or writing it out and placing it in a visible place in your home or work space. Notice when it might be time to choose another mantra.

Practice:

Choose one of these lessons and transform it into a daily practice. For example, meditate with the mantra from the "remember" activity eighty-eight times in one sitting every morning at sunrise. Or something else.

Collaborate:

Brainstorm. Who do you think of as your pod? Try out this pod-mapping worksheet created by Mia Mingus and the Bay Area Transformative Justice Collective: https://batjc .wordpress.com/pods-and-pod-mapping-worksheet/

Do you have multiple pods for multiple situations or different parts of your life? Make a list or as many lists as you need. You may want to do some of the group versions of these activities with some of the people on the list to test them out. #podlife

Be Vulnerable:

We are often most vulnerable in our areas of growth. Out of all the movements of this book, what is the area of growth for you right now? (Respecting your hair? Ending capitalism? Resting?) What would be a brave action for you in relationship to that area of growth? It could look like reaching out for support, if you would usually go it alone. It could look like being compassionate with yourself and making space for your feelings about it. Notice how you feel. Reflect on where the growth is happening in your body, in your relationships, in your work.

Be Present:

Presence in a shifting context takes practice. Marine mammals live in water, a substance that perpetually moves, and moves them/us when it moves. So I offer you this meditation practice:

Choose a marine mammal that is featured in this book and listen to a sound recording of them or watch a video of them. Try to find a recording that is at least five minutes long (humpback whale sounds will most likely be the most broadly accessible). Listening to the marine mammal recording, count your breaths. One inhale and one exhale equals one breath. Count each one. If you lose count, start back at one. Reflect on what you notice.

Be Fierce:

At least one of the refusals in this book can fit on a protest sign or a graphic t-shirt. Make it so.

Learn from Conflict:

Dedicate a passage from this book to someone you are currently in conflict with. If it is not possible or beneficial to actually send them the passage, study it yourself with them in mind. What does this particular passage have to teach you about conflict? How does it reflect the situation you are navigating? Take on the perspective of different figures in the passage, the speaker, the marine mammal, the fishing industry, the scientists, etc. Work with this for three days. What did you learn?

Honor Your Boundaries:

Choose a quotation from this book to use as an outgoing voicemail message or an automatic response email for at least one day. Let it do your explaining for you.

Respect Your Hair:

Using a mirror or your hands, get in touch with one strand of hair on your head, face, or body. Continuing to breathe, stay connected to that one strand of hair. Notice it in relationship to the hairs around it. Like a walrus, ask it what it knows. Write a letter to yourself from the perspective of that one hair. Listen carefully.

End Capitalism:
We can end capitalism one transformed relationship at a time. Choose an aspect of the economic system that entangles marine mammals mentioned in this book and change your relationship to it for a period of at least thirty days. For example, I have a commitment not to eat anything sourced directly from the ocean. Is there one product that fishing boats extract that you can shift your relationship with? Your relationship to oil? To tourism? Shift one relationship for at least thirty days and see what you learn about interconnectedness, complicity, possibility, and freedom.

Refuse:
Inspired by one of the marine mammals featured in the "Refuse" section of this book or in the entire book, choose an area in your life in which to say "no" this week.

Surrender:
If you can, get in some salt water and float on your back for a solid three minutes. If that is not a possibility, choose any of the activities in this section that require you to "choose a passage from the book" and, instead of choosing, open the book randomly to a page and use that passage.

Go deep:
Take one passage from this book and do further research. Deep dive to learn more details about the marine mammals and historical and systemic contexts mentioned. Then ask yourself, how is this passage the story of my own life? Where in your life is this passage the most relevant? Write a guidebook entry about that part of yourself. (For example my workaholism, my relationship to school, my resentful

overgenerosity, my talent for painting.) How would someone identify it? Where is it usually found? What does it look like when it is first born? What feeds it? What threatens it?

Stay Black:
If you are living in the world as a Black person, good job! You have already done so much. Choose a passage in this book, or in the "Stay Black" section in particular, that affirms you, and sing it to yourself, two-step with it, rub some lotion on while you read it. Thank you for being who you are.

If you are living in the world as a non-Black person, ponder the unknowable within yourself. Choose something that living as a non-Black person in an anti-Black world has taught you and decide to unlearn it. Search the Internet for the meaning and context of some of the references in the "Stay Black" section that originate in various Black cultural practices. Learn with reverence.

Slow Down:
Cancel one thing this week. Just one thing. During that time, look at the live-feed of orcas and just see if an orca emerges at any moment.[52] Or go to sleep and let the orca watch you.

Rest:
Take this book to bed with you. Open to any page. Read that passage over and over again until you fall asleep. If you dream, write down your dream. And then read the passage again.

Take Care of Your Blessings:
Make a list of those loves that are sacred to you, those relationships that are closest to your heart at this time. Brainstorm how you can model a form of care exemplified by a marine mammal in this text to each of those loved ones.

---

52 Https://explore.org/livecams/orcas/orcalab-base.

Some examples are snuggling, communicating in a lower frequency, creating physical space, protection, traveling together. Commit or recommit to at least three forms of care, and communicate that commitment in the way that you can to those loved ones.

Activities (Pod/Squad Version):

Choose a friend or two or three, or do these with your organization, workplace, neighbors, fam, etc.:

Listen:

Practice listening. In this exercise each person chooses one of the marine mammal meditations in *Undrowned* and leaves them as a voicemail or voice memo on someone else's phone. What do you hear beyond the words? Offer back a reflection. If you are gathered together in person, form a circle and take turns listening to someone else reading a passage.

This activity should be adaptable based on how the folks in your pod listen. Sharing through tactile sign language, ASL videos, tapping, lip-reading, or hands-to-mouth listening may be appropriate.

Breathe:

As a group, or in a video or audio conference, breathe together. Listen to the sound of your collective breathing while each person breathes at their own pace and attends to their own breath. Notice the particular symphony of your group. Discuss it. Are their rhythms or patterns you notice? Try breathing in unison. See if you can coordinate your inhale and your exhale together, or not. Notice what is hard, easy, surprising, awkward, or resonant about trying to breathe in unison.

Remember:

As a group, choose a mantra from a short phrase in this book that was compelling to one or more of you. You can also create a mantra that combines two or more different phrases that resonated with different people, but it should be short enough that you all can *remember* it. You can chant it as a mantra together or start meetings and gatherings with it. Say it when you see each other in passing. Have fun.

Practice:

Practice practicing. If you did the solo version of this activity and chose an area in which to develop a daily practice, one collaborative step could be to find an accountability buddy to check in with about how keeping to that practice is going, what comes up? What benefits emerge? What obstacles are there to staying with the practice?

Alternatively, with one or more people, you could create a practice that you all do individually or collectively on a regular basis (weekly, monthly, daily, quarterly). Hold each other accountable to your commitment and notice what comes up and what opportunities you have to support each other.

Collaborate:

Clearly doing any of these activities together is an act of collaboration. Take it to another level and work with your pod/squad to create an even more expansive collaboration. This could look like broadening one of the practices you are doing together to a larger collective, collaborating on documenting and sharing what you are doing together, or simply reflecting on how you can support each other more to really manifest what's at the core of this practice for each of you.

Be Vulnerable:

This is an opportunity to go beyond the icebreaker if you are practicing with a group you don't know well, or to unlearn codependent behavior if you are collaborating with people with whom you share a lot of intertwined emotional labor.

In a meeting or retreat this could look like one of my favorite activities ever: the partner haiku or the partner dance.

In this, pairs of people share something from one of their areas of growth. That's the vulnerability, sharing something you haven't figured out yet. After about three minutes you switch and the other partner shares. After both partners have shared you silently write a haiku poem as a reflection, blessing, and offering to the other person. I like to use the three line Haiku with a 5-7-5 syllable structure. But any haiku is fine.

Be Present:

Choose a passage from this book and say it in slow motion together. One person reads slowly and another person speaks the words so closely with them it approaches unison.[53] See what happens.

Be Fierce:

Organize a direct action in relationship to one of the issues mentioned in this book.

Learn from Conflict:

Each person choose a marine mammal and have a principled argument as to which marine mammal is the best and why. Debate for at least one hour. Remember, what makes it a principled argument is love and respect at every moment. What do you notice about your relationship to conflict as you practice love, respect, and disagreement?

Honor Your Boundaries:

Together each person shares three areas of their lives that feel like boundaries that support them, and three areas that feel like borders that constrain them. Using the passages in this section, have a discussion about how you can support each other's boundaries and overcome, defy or challenge the borders that constrain us.

---

53 Love and gratitude to Andrea E. Woods Valdez, who inspired this activity with a dance exercise she taught at Duke University.

Respect Your Hair:
Actually, don't touch my hair. Let's keep this a solo activity.

End Capitalism:
Choose a word that is in this text to say instead of "money" for a week. Hold each other accountable. Check in at the end of the day or the week to see when and where it was difficult. Why?

Refuse:
Boycott or divest from something together informed by the economic systems that threaten marine mammals and all of us. Publicize it and make space for people to join you.

Surrender:
Round one: Offer each other assignments based on passages of this book. Accept, reject, or modify the assignment you receive. Notice as a collective how it feels to accept or reject or modify an assignment. Notice and reflect on how it feels to have your assignment accepted or rejected or modified.

Round two (optional): Offer each other assignments based on passages of this book, with the agreement that everyone will accept their assignment as is.

Go deep:
With a partner, choose a topic that you *want* to go deeper into. Explain it. Your partner will ask you "what's under that?" and you will continue to respond with another layer of how the topic occurs for you. Repeat at least seven times. And then switch.

Stay Black:
Create tangible gifts for each other or for other Black people informed by this book.

Slow Down:

Choose a passage from this book and read it together one word at a time, taking turns. Go around the circle with each person reading one word until you have read all of the words. What do you notice?

Rest:

Choose a collectively rejuvenating activity... Or practice giving each other a break?

Take Care of Your Blessings:

Tell the group about someone you cherish. Brainstorm together about how you can deepen your care for that person. Each person should leave the session with at least one action they can take to deepen their care, make it more sustainable, bless it with boundaries.

In case you are wondering, yes, the author is totally interested in finding out about how your exploration of these activities went. Reach out to @alexispauline on Twitter or Instagram or the descendants of Twitter and Instagram.